1. *Criminal Law for OCR AS*

with an introduction to the nature of law

Sally Russell LLB (Hons), PGCE

Key features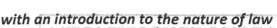

- **Tasks** a__ s__f-te_t questions thro_g____ (with answers __ y___r __ _.org)

- **Key cases with key principles highlighted**

- **Examples to bring the law to life**

- **Summaries with diagrams for the main points of each area**

- **Links between the criminal law and the nature of law**

- **Examination and evaluation pointers**

- **Examination guidance and question practice**

- **Free interactive exercises at www.drsr.org**

My main objective has been to combine legal accuracy with a style that is accessible to all students, so I hope you will find this book both stimulating and helpful. Fully updated with recent cases and laws it is written in a lively, clear and accessible way and is designed to help students of all learning styles to understand the subject.

The tasks and clear explanations mean the book can be used in the classroom or as a self-study guide.

Other books by Sally Russell

As new books may be available by the time you read this, I have not listed my other books by title. They currently include crime and tort at AS and A level for both the AQA and OCR examination boards. Also, 'the law explained' series offers a more in-depth coverage of individual areas with additional tasks, examples and examination practice. These cover much of crime and tort as well as the various concepts of law. This means you can pick those topics for which you need more guidance (all the answers to tasks are included in the booklets).

For the most up to date list of what is available, please check my author's page on Amazon or visit my website at www.drsr.org. All my books are available in both Kindle and paperback.

Table of contents

Introduction...1

An introduction to Criminal law for Year 1 A level and AS 3

Chapter 1: The Nature of Law and the Rule of law..4

The nature of law..4

The rule of law 7

Chapter 2: Actus reus: Conduct, circumstances, consequences and causation 11

Conduct...11

Consequences and causation..14

Chapter 3 Mens rea..20

Intention 20

Recklessness 24

Chapter 4 Strict liability...28

Statutory nature of strict liability..28

Interpretation by the courts..29

social utility (usefulness) and public policy 30

Arguments for and against imposing strict liability...31

Chapter 5 Common assault: Assault and Battery 35

Assault 35

Battery 38

Consent 38

Chapter 6 Assault occasioning actual bodily harm (ABH) under s 47 of the Offences against the Person Act 1861 42

Actus reus 42

Mens rea...44

Chapter 7 Grievous bodily harm (GBH) and wounding under s 20 and s 18 of the Offences against the Person Act 1861 47

Actus reus for s 18 and s 20 47

Mens rea for s 20..50

Mens rea for s 18..50

Summary: Non-fatal offences against the person **54**

Evaluation: Problems and proposals for reform of the non-fatal offences..................................*55*

Chapter 8: Examination practice for AS **57**

About the examination *57*

The assessment objectives (AOs) 57

Types of question and apportionment of marks 57

Examination guidance *57*

Application advice 57

Evaluation advice...59

Examination paper for AS...*61*

Chapter 9: The Bridge...**62**

Evaluation of the non-fatal offences against the person and proposals for reform........................*62*

Background of proposed reforms *63*

The Law Commission Report (No 361) 2015..*63*

The nature of law (concepts) *64*

Appendix: Abbreviations and acknowledgements...**71**

Index of cases **72**

Introduction

This book covers the criminal law for OCR AS, as well as an introduction to the nature of law. AS criminal law is the same as the first year of A level criminal law. If you are doing the full A level then Criminal Law for OCR AS and A level is better for you as it covers both the AS and the additional material required for the A level.

This book introduces you to the nature of law and then covers the five non-fatal offences against the person. This is the material you need for both AS and A level criminal law.

More on how the key features can help:

- **Examples help you to see how the law relates to real life situations**

- **Tasks and self-test questions help you to check your understanding**

- **Links between the criminal law and the nature of law help you to see how the law relates to concepts such as justice and morality**

- **Examination pointers help with application**

- **Evaluation pointers help you to see problems with the law**

- **Key cases show you the important cases to know, and where a principle of law is established this is clearly stated**

- **Summaries and diagrams help to make the law clear and accessible**

After the coverage of the offences there is a chapter on examination practice followed by a full examination paper. This is only needed for AS students, there is no need to take an external examination at the end of Year 1 if you are doing the full A level.

It is a bit early to talk about examinations (covered in depth in Chapter 8) but there are a couple of things you need to know now so you can use the book effectively.

In some questions, you will be asked to apply the law to a set of facts, in others to evaluate it. There are 'pointers' throughout the book to help with this.

Examination pointers

These relate to legal rules and application of the law. For application of the law you need to identify the specific legal rules that apply to the given facts. Then you need to apply those rules logically to the facts in order to reach a sustainable conclusion. You will need to support what you say by using cases and principles to illustrate your points and then reach a conclusion based on your application.

The law for application is the current law and latest case developments.

Evaluation pointers

These cover criticisms of the law. They are for evaluation questions where you may be asked to provide a critique of the law on a particular topic or a particular legal rule. Any problems with the law will also suggest that the rule of law is not being upheld or justice not achieved as both these concepts require fairness and clarity. The evaluation pointer may show the law has improved in some way, too, as any critique should include the good points. The law for evaluation may need to include developments or advantages and disadvantages, not just the latest cases and principles.

Try to produce a balanced argument. Where there is debate on an issue there are usually valid arguments on both sides, so don't strive to write what you think examiners want to see; they will be much more impressed by independent thought. Have an opinion, but look at the issue from the other point of view too to show that you have considered the arguments before reaching that opinion.

A final few things before you start your studies.

It is important to try to learn plenty of cases as these help to show you how the law works in practice. If you have trouble remembering them then do the best you can, but be sure that you at least know the 'key cases' well.

Criminal cases are usually in the form *R v the defendant (D)*. It is acceptable to use just the name so if the case is **R v Miller** I have called it **Miller**. If another form is used, e.g., **DPP v Miller** I have used the full title, as you may want to look up the case for further information.

Civil cases are between the *claimant* (C) and the *defendant* (D), although you will still see the use of the old word *'plaintiff'* in cases before 1999, when it changed to *'claimant'*.

There is a list of some common abbreviations in the appendix at the end of the book.

Chapter 1 covers the rule of law and some general principles of law. It also introduces you to the nature of law. This includes the differences between legal and other rules and the concepts of morality and justice. These are part of the English legal system but are covered here to help you to relate these concepts to the criminal law in this book.

Chapters 2 and 3 cover the basic general principles specific to criminal liability. These apply to the all the offences contained in the AS and A level course.

Chapters 5, 6 and 7 cover five different non-fatal offences against the person (also needed for both AS and A level). These are:

- **Assault – where D (the defendant) puts someone in fear of harm**

- **Battery – where D uses force on someone**

- **Actual bodily harm (ABH) – when either of the above causes an injury which isn't serious**

- **Grievous bodily harm (GBH) or wounding – where someone suffers serious harm or a cut**

- **Grievous bodily harm or wounding with intent – where someone suffers serious harm or a cut which D intended**

These offences are commonly called 'the assaults'. However, they are separate and distinct offences, with different rules on each.

Example

Jane threatens Jenny and then pushes her. Jenny is scared and runs away. She trips and grazes her knee. Frightening Jenny is assault, pushing her is battery. Jenny grazed her knee which is actual bodily harm. If she is seriously hurt or cut badly it will be grievous bodily harm or wounding. If Jane *intended* to harm Jenny seriously, it would be grievous bodily harm or wounding with intent.

There is some evaluation of these offences in the chapters covering them and more in the summary following the offences

Chapter 8 covers examination practice and a full examination paper.

The last chapter is The Bridge. This contains more evaluation and more on the nature of law. The connections between law and morality, and law and justice are included in the AS specifications but more depth is needed for A level. The Bridge gives you a taster in case you decide to continue with your studies. If you don't you can ignore the last chapter as regards the nature of law, but you may find the extra evaluation useful for AS if you aim to achieve top grades.

The word law in phrases such as criminal law, human rights law, contract law etc., refers to the substance of the law (hence these topics are called substantive law). The word law in a wider sense is a more elusive concept, as it relates to the nature rather than the substance of law (called non-substantive law). It involves consideration of what academics and judges think the nature of law is (and what it should be). This in itself involves consideration of theories of law, such as law and justice, law and morality, the role of law in society in balancing competing interests and the role of law in keeping up with and regulating new technology. When considering the nature of law you need to look at the rest of your course from a different perspective.

The nature of law is a very wide term. In one sense it covers the theory of law regarding where law comes from, differences between civil and criminal liability and differences between legal rules and other types of rule. It also covers the rule of law. In another, more specific sense it covers legal theories, or concepts of law. I have included an introduction to the nature of law in this book so you can see how these theories relate to the cases you will learn. All these are part of the English legal system although the specific concepts are not needed in depth for AS. There is therefore an introduction here and more detail in The Bridge.

The nature of law (general theory)

The nature of law is essentially that it is based on rules. Legal liability occurs when the rules have been broken. In order to understand the nature of law we need to know a bit more about where the law comes from, what distinguishes a legal rule from other rules (or norms) of behaviour, how a person may become liable in law and what differences there are between civil and criminal liability.

Sources of Law

We are governed by rules imposed by the state. This includes the courts, which produce common law through cases heard in court, and Parliament which produces statute law. Some (not many) laws come from custom, i.e., they have been going on for so long they are accepted as law even though not set out in a case or statute. Equity is a source of law which developed alongside the common law. It is not seen so much today and is mostly connected to the civil law (e.g., an injunction is an equitable remedy and is an alternative to the normal remedy of monetary compensation). These are all sources of law. Other sources of law today include European law and Human rights law.

All these areas are covered elsewhere in the course under the English legal system.

Legal rules and criminal liability

Social rules are often referred to as norms. A norm can be described as the expected standard of behaviour within a society. However both legal rules (law) and social rules (morals) are called norms by academics and lawyers. That is why it is important to be able to differentiate between law and morals (see the nature of law below). It is possible to say all rules are norms, but social norms are not enforced in a court of law whereas legal norms are.

There is no agreed definition of law. Essentially, it is a matter of rules, but so is much a life. Therefore, a distinction needs to be made between enforceable legal rules and other norms of behaviour. There are many rules governing our lives but not all are enforceable. There may be rules governing how you behave in school or college, and there will be rules at home too. None of these rules has the force of law. A teacher or parent may punish (sanction) you for breaking these rules but there will be no such sanctions from a court of law.

Law is based on liability. A person is legally liable when accountable in law for something done/not done. There are two types of liability, criminal and civil, and both are based on the principle of individuals being responsible for their conduct.

- Criminal liability is based on an individual's responsibility to the state and society as a whole
- Civil liability is based on an individual's responsibility to other individuals

The main differences between criminal and civil liability are seen in the *consequences* not the deed. Harming someone is against the criminal law, but the victim (V) may want to sue in civil law to claim compensation for any injuries, thus there is both criminal and civil liability. Here is a summary of the different types of action in court:

Criminal Law

- **Proceedings are initiated by the Crown (Crown Prosecution Service)**
- **Proceedings are paid for by the State**
- **Cases commence in the Magistrates' Court**
- **Serious crimes are heard in the Crown Court**
- **The accused is prosecuted**
- **The burden of proof is on the prosecution**
- **The standard of proof is beyond reasonable doubt**
- **The primary purpose is punishment**
- **The case is in the form of R v Smith (R stands for Regina i.e., the Crown)**

Civil Law

- **Proceedings are initiated by the individual (the claimant)**
- **Proceedings are paid for by the parties (usually the loser)**
- **Cases commence in the County Court or High Court depending on the amount claimed**
- **The defendant is sued**
- **The burden of proof is on the Claimant**
- **The standard of proof is the balance of probabilities**
- **The primary purpose is compensation, called damages**
- **The case is in the form of Smith v Brown (i.e., the parties to the dispute)**

If you prefer diagrams:

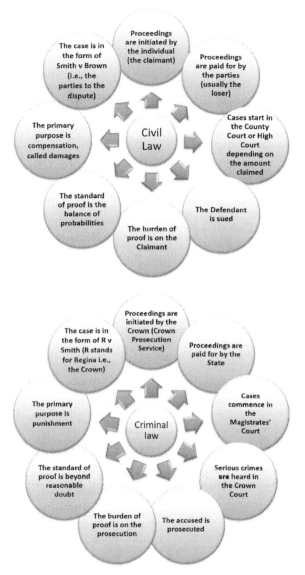

As this book deals with the criminal law a little more on the background of criminal liability is needed. There is no exact definition of a crime, but there are some fundamental principles which are accepted as being part of the nature of criminal law. The criminal law **prohibits** certain actions and **punishes** those who commit them.

The basic elements of criminal liability are **guilty conduct** (known as *actus reus*) and **guilty mind** (known as *mens rea*). These general elements of liability are dealt with in the next two Chapters. When making rules of criminal law certain principles are upheld. One principle is that the law, especially criminal law, must be certain and the rules clearly defined. This is a requirement of both the rule of law and justice. It is often referred to as 'fair labelling' and you will come to see that there are several offences that are not sufficiently clearly defined, in particular the non-fatal offences against the person.

The main basis for criminalising behaviour is harm. This is not only harm to a person but also harm to property, hence laws **prohibiting** violence and theft. The law expects people to be responsible for their actions, so **punishes** those who break the law if found to be at fault. This is the principle of individual autonomy. Individuals are deemed responsible for their own behaviour and this justifies imposing punishment on them for breaking the rules. There are different levels of fault in criminal law, and these are covered in Chapter 3.

Whatever the level of fault (*mens rea*), it is generally accepted that it should correspond with the conduct (*actus reus*) so that a person should only be criminally liable where the *mens rea* was for the offence actually committed. This principle is called the correspondence principle but you will come to see that it is not always followed in practice. Where there is no accordance, or correspondence, between the *actus reus* and *mens rea* it is known as constructive liability and you will see examples of this with the substantive law as it applies to two of the non-fatal offences against the person (as well as murder and manslaughter).

Finally, it is generally accepted that the law should not be retrospective; it should apply to the future and not the past. This is the case with statute law passed by Parliament as that will prohibit behaviour from the time the Act becomes law. However, with the common law, which comes from judgments in cases, this is not always true because if the decision has changed the law, the person in court maybe guilty of something that was not previously illegal (an example is the case of **R v R** discussed in detail in The Bridge).

Note: There are still a few Latin terms used in law. Don't worry, they seem scary at first but you will be using them so often they will soon seem familiar.

The nature of law (specific concepts)

The nature of law includes how law operates in society, involving different theories (or concepts) of law. These will be covered in depth in my book on human rights and the nature of law, as legal theory is a subject in its own right. However, the concepts need to be related to all areas of study and although they will not be tested in depth at AS you need to have a basic understanding of them. It is therefore a good idea to think about them, at least briefly, as you work through the book. Thus, if you see a case which you think was decided unfairly you can ask yourself whether the law is achieving justice or upholding the rule of law. I have therefore included a short introduction here, followed by a note on how you can link the concepts to the law.

Law and morality – as noted when looking at rules, the law only punishes someone for breaking legal rules, not social (or moral) ones. However, legal rules sometimes overlap with social rules and morality. This is what law and morality is about: how far social and legal rules overlap and whether the law should be involved in moral issues. Sometimes the law has to get involved because a moral issue comes up in court (examples are whether life support can be withdrawn from a patient in a coma and whether an anorexic teenager could be force-fed against her wishes).

Law and justice – justice is in the very nature of law, so there are many examples throughout this book of whether the legal rules on a specific area achieve justice. The rule of law (see below) is similar as it requires fairness and equality and both these are also in the nature of justice, at least to most people. One formal view of justice (called positivism) is that justice depends on legal rules. A law that is made properly using the correct procedures will be a just law whether or not it is moral. Another view of justice (called natural law) is that it is based on moral rules, so if a law is not moral it is not a true law. This shows the overlap between justice and morality.

The rule of law is discussed below in detail because it applies to both AS and A level law. This concept contains many of the elements required by justice and many cases could be used to illustrate both these concepts. When you look at these consider two questions:

■ **Is the legal system just (procedural justice)?**

■ **Is a particular law just (substantive justice)?**

Law and society – The law plays a role in society by way of social control. One method of controlling people's behaviour is to make laws regulating it. In doing this the law needs to balance competing interests, those of society and those of individuals within that society. There are many laws regulating behaviour that are civil rather than criminal matters. However, many can involve both types of law, such as health and safety regulations where a breach of the rules can lead to a civil claim for negligence and a criminal prosecution. The law also has to balance conflicting interests when dealing with disputes between the parties in a court case.

Law and technology – As technology improves (or even if it doesn't improve but just changes) the law will need to be ready for this. Advanced medical techniques can lead to a new procedure which hasn't been possible before and may need the intervention of the law in the case of disputes. An example is the embryology technique that allows for the cloning of embryos. This has led to several court cases and a new Act of Parliament to regulate the new procedures. Other examples include cyber-crime, on-line abuse, data protection and internet grooming. These issues mostly come into human rights law. For negligence, examples are the use of drones and driverless cars, or robot-controlled procedures. These may lead to cases of negligence but there is the question of who the claim will be against – you cannot sue a robot! Drones used for deliveries are already the subject of complaints from people who say they have been a nuisance (flying too close, landing in the wrong garden etc.). Nuisance is a tort in its own right which is studied for A level but not AS.

Linking the concepts with the law

I have added a link at the end of each chapter which gives you a hint as to how the law in that chapter could relate to a concept. This is very brief because AS students are not expected to discuss specific theories in depth. However you could be asked to evaluate an area and to comment on whether justice is achieved. There is more detail in The Bridge in case you decide to continue. In order to explain a theory you need to use case examples to illustrate what you say. Paper 3, 'Further Law', requires you to use examples from across the whole course, including the AS topics.

Both justice and the rule of law require fairness and clarity so there are many cases which can be used to illustrate these concepts. The overlap between concepts can be seen in the case example in Task 1. The law controlled the way people behaved by making the behaviour illegal. The interests of the people involved (to do what they wanted in private) were balanced against the fact that the law need to protect people from violence. The public interest was seen as more important so they were found guilty. The case is also an example of the law enforcing morality. The decision was partly based on morality as some of the judges thought society itself was harmed by allowing such behaviour, even in private. Under the natural law view of justice the decision was correct as the behaviour was arguably immoral. Under the positivist view of justice that would not matter: a positivist would agree with the decision being based on the legal rule not to cause serious harm intentionally. This was an appeal case heard in the House of Lords by five judges. The decision was a 3-2 majority. You can see that even the judges in the case disagreed on what justice was and whether it was achieved.

This first task gives you an idea of how you might think about these concepts as you read a particular case.

Task 1

In **Brown 1994**, serious injuries had occurred during consensual sado-masochistic sex in private. This was a criminal case and those involved were convicted of grievous bodily harm. They were all adults and no-one was forced to participate, but the court decided that the defence of consent could not be applied to serious harm where it was intentional. One judge said that the public should be protected from violence and that society itself was harmed by such behaviour, even if it happened in private. Another judge said it was not for the courts to protect people from themselves.

Briefly explain how the nature of law played a role in this case (justice, morality and social control).

The rule of law

The rule of law is part of the English legal system but it is relevant to all other areas of law and legal procedure.

When rules of law and procedure are formulated they should conform to the rule of law. This involves equality, clarity and fairness.

- **The law should apply to everyone equally and no-one should be above the law.**

- **The law must be clear so that people know the rules (then if the rules are broken it will be fair to punish those at fault).**

- **The law must be accessible so that if a person is accused of a crime it is only fair that access to justice and legal advice is possible.**

This is a simplified description of the rule of law, and it applies not only to Paper 1 at AS but also to Paper 3 for the A level, so needs further discussion.

The Rule of Law

The **Constitutional Reform Act 2005** refers to the rule of law, and the Lord Chancellor's oath requires the Lord Chancellor to respect the rule of law, but there is no agreed definition of it. An early view of the rule of law is that formulated by Dr Thomas Fuller in 1733: "Be you ever so high, the law is above you". This view has continued for centuries. In **Evans v AG 2015**, the SC ruled that correspondence between Prince Charles and government ministers should be made public under the **Freedom of**

Information Act and said it was "fundamental to the rule of law" that decisions and actions of the executive are subject to review in a court of law.

The rule of law was popularised by A. V. Dicey (a constitutional lawyer) in the following century. He said, in summary, "everyone, whatever his rank, is subject to the ordinary law of the land". A little more recently, Lord Bingham said "If you maltreat a penguin in the London zoo, you do not escape prosecution because you are the Archbishop of Canterbury". So, an important part of the rule of law is that everyone is subject to it, with no exceptions. There is more to it than that, and opinions differ on what it means in the modern sense. Although the rule of law is a somewhat abstract notion, to try to explain it today a good place to start is with Lord Bingham's 2014 lecture on the subject, taken from his book 'The Rule of Law'. The core principle is as above, that no-one is above the law, including those who make it. He notes that the rule of law has evolved and continues to do so, and sets out eight sub-rules which he feels describe the rule of law in its current form. These are:

Law must be accessible. This means that if people are bound by the law they must be able to know what the law is.

Questions of legal rights and liabilities should be resolved by application of the law and not be a matter of discretion. This does not mean there is absolutely no discretion. A judge must exercise a certain amount of discretion when deciding on an appropriate sentence or remedy – the point is that any such discretion is limited by law, e.g., statutes or earlier decisions.

The law should apply equally to all. This is accepted by most people as being part of any rule of law but Lord Bingham points out that in practice it is not always apparent. An example is the various **Terrorism Acts** where non-nationals suspected of terrorism are subject to being locked up without trial, but nationals are not – even though they pose the same threat. It is arguable that anyone subject to national laws should be entitled to the law's protection. Even where the law appears to apply equally it may not in practice. It is true that the Archbishop of Canterbury is not above the law – but if he does mistreat a penguin he can probably afford a decent lawyer to help his case! The **Legal Aid, Sentencing and Punishment of Offenders Act 2012 (LASPO)**, has severely reduced access to justice and legal aid, especially in civil cases.

The law should adequately protect fundamental human rights. This is perhaps a more recent addition to the concept of the rule of law. The preamble to the **Universal Declaration of Human Rights** says that if people are not to be compelled to rebel against tyranny and oppression that "human rights should be protected by the rule of law".

The state must meet its obligations under international law. Thus an act by a state that is unlawful would be against the rule of law. He referred to the war against Iraq and whilst not saying whether or not he believed it to be illegal, he did say that if it *was* illegal then it would be against the rule of law "if this sub-rule is sound".

Means must be provided for resolving civil disputes. He says that if people are bound by the law they should receive its benefits and should be able to go to court to have their rights and liberties determined "in the last resort". He does not rule out less formal methods of resolving disputes but sees access to the courts as a "basic right" adding that legal advice should be affordable and available without excessive delay. Where the first sub-rule requires law to be accessible in the sense of clarity, this sub-rule requires accessibility in terms of cost. It has been said that justice is open to all "like the Ritz hotel" – meaning that everyone may be entitled to it but many are unable to use it in practice due to lack of money. Going back to the mistreatment of penguins, the Archbishop is more likely to be able to afford to go to the Ritz and to gain access to justice than the average person on the street is, especially since **LASPO.**

All public officials must exercise their power reasonably and not exceed its limits. As with the second rule, this rule is against the arbitrary use of power. An example of its application is that everyone has the right to apply for judicial review of a decision made by public officers and government ministers – a judge cannot overturn such a decision, but can rule that it is unreasonable.

Adjudicative procedures must be fair. This means open court hearings, the right to be heard, the right to know what the charges and evidence against you are, that the decision maker is independent and impartial, and that in criminal cases D is innocent until guilt is proved. Fairness would also cover access to justice in both the earlier senses of clarity and cost.

Lord Bingham sees the rule of law as depending on an unspoken bargain between the individual and the state. The citizen sacrifices some freedom by accepting legal constraints on certain activities, and the state sacrifices some power by recognising it cannot do all that it has the power to do. He concludes that this means those who maintain and protect the rule of law are "guardians of an all but sacred flame which animates and enlightens the society in which we live".

To sum up the rule of law:

No-one is above the law

Everyone is subject to the law, not the arbitrary exercise of power

The law must encompass clarity, access to justice, fairness and an independent and impartial judiciary

The law must apply equally

In Lord Bingham's view, the rule of law should also protect human rights and comply with international obligations if it is to apply to a modern state with national and international commitments. Bear that in mind if you will be studying human rights for Paper 3.

As you study the law try to consider whether the rule of law is being upheld.

Task 2

Explain what Lord Bingham meant when he said "If you maltreat a penguin in the London zoo, you do not escape prosecution because you are the Archbishop of Canterbury". Add a comment of your own as to whether you agree that this should be part of the rule of law.

Self-test questions

2. *State two sources of law*

3. *State three differences between civil and criminal law*

4. *What is the core principle of the rule of law?*

5. *What is the legal term for guilty conduct?*

6. *What is the legal term for a guilty mind?*

Chapter 2: Actus reus: *Conduct, circumstances, consequences and causation*

"... there was gross and criminal negligence, as the man was paid to keep the gate shut and protect the public ... a man might incur criminal liability from a duty arising out of a contract". Wright J

By the end of this Chapter, you should be able to:

- Explain *actus reus* in relation to conduct, omissions and circumstances

- Explain how *actus reus* may involve consequences

- Illustrate how causation is proved by reference to cases

- Identify possible criticisms for an evaluation of the law

There are two elements which need to be proved for most offences. These are known by the Latin terms *actus reus* and *mens rea*. *Mens rea* involves the state of mind of D (the defendant) at the time of the offence and we will deal with this in Chapter 3. First, we will look at *actus reus* which involves everything else (other than the mental element), which makes up the crime.

These two Chapters are important because these basic requirements for criminal liability are needed for the other offences you will study.

It is very important to identify each element of the *actus reus* of a crime because there can be no crime unless the *actus reus* is complete. This does not necessarily mean D will be acquitted. If part of the *actus reus* of an offence is not proved then *that* offence is not committed, but there may well be a connected offence or an attempt.

Although in simple terms *actus reus* means a guilty act or wrongful conduct, there is more to it than this. It may include:

- conduct (which is voluntary)

- circumstances

- a consequence (which is caused by D's conduct)

Conduct

Conduct can consist of an act, an omission, or a state of affairs. An **act** is usually straightforward, e.g., hitting someone. As a rule, the conduct must be voluntary. This is seen in **Leicester v Pearson 1952** where a car driver was prosecuted for failing to give precedence to a pedestrian on a zebra crossing. It was shown that his car had been pushed onto the crossing by another car hitting him from behind. He was acquitted. He had not acted voluntarily. An **omission** is a failure to act. In criminal law, this will not usually make you guilty unless you have a duty to act in the first place. An example is failing to look after your child. A **state of affairs** is where you can commit an offence just by being in a certain state, e.g., 'being *drunk* in charge of a motor vehicle'. In these cases the conduct may not be voluntary.

Acts and omissions

In **Fagan v Metropolitan Police Commissioner 1969**, D accidentally drove onto a police officer's foot whilst parking. He didn't move his car when asked; in fact, he used some fairly colourful language which I will not repeat here. He was promptly arrested for, and convicted of, assaulting a police officer in the execution of his duty. He argued that there was no *mens rea* at the time of the act (driving onto his foot) and that the refusal to move was only an omission, not an act. The court held that there was a *continuing act* which started with the driving onto the police officer's foot and continued up to the refusal to move. Thus, not moving when asked to was part of the original act rather than an omission. At this time, he did have *mens rea*. Having decided that this type of assault could not be committed by omission, the CA used the idea of a continuing act to overcome the problem. This case also reaffirms the point that *actus reus* and *mens rea* must be contemporaneous (i.e., coincide or happen at the same time).

A case illustrating the distinction between an act and an omission is **Airedale NHS Trust v Bland 1993**. Tony Bland, who was 17, had been badly injured in the Hillsborough football stadium disaster. He was in what is called a persistent vegetative state and had no hope of recovery. The family and doctors wanted to stop treatment, including artificial feeding. The HL confirmed a court order allowing this. They drew a distinction between a positive act that killed (such as administering a lethal injection) which could never be lawful, and an omission to act which allowed someone to die (e.g., not providing life-saving treatment).

The cases of **Diane Pretty** and **Ms B** in **2002** also illustrate this distinction. In the first, Mrs Pretty wanted her husband to help her commit suicide and took her case to the HL and then the European Court of Human Rights. She wanted a court order that he would not be prosecuted for assisting her suicide. She failed, as this would be a positive act. In the latter case, Ms B wanted treatment discontinued and succeeded in obtaining a court order to allow this, even though it meant she would die. In both cases the women were terminally ill. There have been many other cases since these as the euthanasia issue is a controversial one. These are outside the scope of this book but illustrate law and morals and balancing interests.

So, there is generally no criminal liability for *not* doing something. However, exceptions occur when there is a duty to act. A duty can occur when:

- Parliament has expressly provided for it by statute
- there is a contractual duty
- a relationship of responsibility gives rise to a common law duty
- D has created a dangerous situation.

In these cases, an omission to act is enough.

Example

You see someone drowning and you are a good swimmer, but leave the person to die. You are not guilty of any crime. However, as I said above, there are exceptions. I will come back to this as we look at the exceptions.

Statutory duty to act

An example is the **Road Traffic Act 1988,** which makes it an offence for a driver involved in a road accident to fail to stop and give a name and address when asked, or to fail to report the accident to the police. There is a duty to stop, and to report the accident, so failing to do so (an omission) is part of the *actus reus* of each of these offences. The **Wireless Telegraphy Act 1949** makes broadcasting without a licence illegal, thus in **Blake 1997**, a disc jockey was convicted under this **Act** for failing to get a licence. The same would apply to failing to have a TV licence.

Contractual duty to act

In **Pittwood 1902**, D was employed as a gatekeeper by a railway company. His job was to keep the gate at the crossing shut whenever a train passed. One day he forgot to close the gate. A hay cart crossed the track and was hit by an oncoming train. One person was killed and another seriously injured. D was under a contractual duty of employment to keep the gates to the crossing shut and to safeguard people using the crossing. His failure to act was in breach of his contractual duty and so amounted to the *actus reus* of manslaughter. The quote at the beginning came from this case.

In my example, if you were a lifeguard you would have a contractual duty to act if you saw someone drowning so could be liable.

Similar to this is a duty where you hold a public office. Thus in **Dytham 1979**, a police officer who failed to act when he saw D kicking someone to death was liable. Here though, he was not guilty of homicide, only of misconduct in a public office.

Relationship of responsibility

In **Stone and Dobinson 1977**, a couple had a relative (Fanny) come and live with them. She was anorexic, and often took to her bed for days at a time, refusing food and any other form of assistance. Her condition seriously deteriorated and after inadequate efforts to obtain medical assistance, she was found dead in her bed. The court held that Stone and Dobinson had undertaken the duty of caring for her and they had been grossly negligent in their failure to fulfil their duty. This failure had caused Fanny's death and so they were guilty of manslaughter.

*In my example, if you were the parent of the swimmer you would have a duty to act so could be liable. You would also have a duty to act if you had taken on responsibility for them, as in **Dobinson**.*

Creating a dangerous situation

In **Miller 1983**, D was squatting in an unoccupied house. One night he fell asleep whilst smoking. When he awoke he realised he'd set fire to the mattress but did nothing to extinguish it, he merely moved to another room. The house caught fire and damage was caused. He was convicted of arson under **s 1 Criminal Damage Act 1971**. The HL upheld his conviction on the basis that if a defendant has unintentionally caused an event, and then realises what has happened, he has a duty to take appropriate action.

In my example, if you pushed the person in, you created the dangerous situation so have a duty to take appropriate action. Again, you could be liable.

Task 3

Compare **Fagan** and **Miller**. Could Miller have been found guilty on the 'continuing act' theory?

State of affairs

A few crimes can be committed without any apparent voluntary act by the accused. In **Larsonneur 1933**, a Frenchwoman was deported against her will from Ireland and brought to England by the police. She was convicted under the **Aliens Order 1920** of being found in the UK without permission. The state of affairs amounting to the *actus reus* was 'being found', so as soon as she landed in the UK without the required permission she committed the offence. This law has since been repealed but a similar situation is seen in **Winzar v Chief Constable of Kent 1983**. A drunk was told to leave a hospital and didn't. He was removed by the police who put him in their car, which was parked on the highway. The police then arrested him for being found drunk on the highway, for which he was later convicted. The state of 'being found' was again enough. So, we can see that 'state of affairs' crimes can occur where something which is normally legal may not be so in certain circumstances. Being drunk is legal, but being drunk 'on the highway' or drunk 'in charge of a motor vehicle' (a state of affairs), is not.

Evaluation pointer

Think about whether there should be liability for omissions. Use the cases above to support your arguments. There is no 'right' answer. It can be argued that there is a moral duty to act if it will save a life. Consider whether there should also be a legal duty. Do you think the court made the right decision in **Airedale NHS Trust v Bland 1993**? It can be said that turning off the machine was an act, but the court viewed it as an omission. On the other hand, in **Fagan v Metropolitan Police Commissioner 1969,** it could be said there was only an omission but the court found a 'continuing act'.

In addition, the 'state of affairs' cases can be criticised. One of the arguments for imposing liability without having to prove fault is that it saves lengthy investigations and court time, but is it fair to D? Should someone be convicted just for being in the wrong place at the wrong time as in Winzar v Chief Constable of Kent 1983 and Larsonneur 1933? Compare these cases to **Leicester v Pearson 1952**.

Circumstances

Many crimes are committed only if the conduct is carried out in particular circumstances. The *actus reus* of theft is the appropriation (taking) of property belonging to another. 'Appropriation' is the conduct, that it is 'property' and 'belongs to another' are both circumstances. *All* these must be proved or it is not theft. Many of the offences against the person have the word 'unlawful' in their definition. If, for example, D acted in self-defence then in these circumstances the act is not unlawful. The *actus reus* is not satisfied.

Task 4 (there is no answer guide for this)

Make a separate folder for the more detailed material you need for the evaluation part of extended writing questions. As you read cases start to question whether the law achieves justice and add your thoughts to the folder. Look out for articles from newspapers or law journals on any of the issues you are discussing. Cut them out and put them in the folder, adding a few of your own comments.

Consequences and causation

Crimes where a particular consequence is part of the *actus reus* are called **result crimes**. Murder is an example. For a murder conviction, death must result from D's act. Homicide is the unlawful killing of a human being. The *actus reus* involves not just killing (conduct) but also that it is unlawful and of a human being (circumstances) and that death occurs (the consequence).

As well as the consequence itself, it must be proved that D's act *caused* this consequence. Many of the cases on causation involve a homicide because it is a result crime. However, even though the principle may come from a murder case it will apply to a case of ABH as that is also a result crime (the assault must cause the bodily harm). The prosecution must prove causation both **factually** and **legally**.

Factual causation

Factual causation is traditionally referred to as the *'sine qua non'* rule. This phrase is defined in Chambers as 'an indispensable condition'. It means D's action must be a *'sine qua non'* or an 'indispensable condition' of the result. More simply put, the result would not have occurred without D's action. It is more commonly called the 'but for' test. The prosecution must show that 'but for' D's conduct, the victim (V) would not have died (or been injured).

Key case

In **White 1910**, D put cyanide in a drink intending to kill his mother, who was found dead shortly afterwards with the drink 3 parts full. In fact, the mother had died of a heart attack unconnected with the poison. The son was found not guilty of murder. He had the *mens rea* (he intended to kill her) but not the *actus reus* (his act didn't cause her death). He didn't get away with it altogether though; he was guilty of attempted murder.

Principle: If the result would have occurred regardless of D's act then D's act did not cause that result.

White illustrates the situation where D's act has *not* factually caused death. Any of the following cases on legal causation could also be used for illustrating causation in fact. As you read them, ask the question: 'but for D's act would V have died / been injured?' If the answer is 'no' then causation in fact is shown. Causation in fact can be very wide.

Example

I ask a college student to stay on for half an hour to finish a project. She therefore misses her bus and walks home. On the way, she is attacked and injured. It can be argued that 'but for' my asking her to stay late she would not have been attacked and so I am liable for her injury. To avoid such a wide liability the courts have built up some rules on how far someone should be liable for the consequences of their actions. This is causation in law.

Legal causation

This is based on what is called the 'chain of causation'. It means proving an unbroken link, or chain, between D's action and the result, for example, death in homicide cases. When something has occurred after D's original act, then it may be argued that the chain of causation is broken. We will look at some cases to explain how this works, but in summary; the chain of causation will not be broken if:

- D's action makes a 'significant' contribution to the result (**Smith/Cheshire**)

- any intervening act was foreseeable (**Roberts**)

- V has a particular weakness and the result would not have occurred in a normal person. This is known as the 'thin skull' rule (**Blaue**)

In my example, I will argue that the chain has been broken by the attacker. I did not make a significant contribution to the harm, and the attack was not foreseeable. I have not legally caused the injuries.

Task 5 (the answer is included below)

Use my example above, but this time you should apply the rules to the attacker. Decide whether the attacker legally caused death in the following situations:

1. The attacker left her badly injured and lying in the road. She is run over by a car and killed.

2. The attacker left her badly injured but a passer-by sees her and calls an ambulance. She is taken to hospital and starts to recover. However, the treatment is wrong and she dies.

3. She was only slightly injured but (not a good day!) she is struck by lightning as she recovers from the attack.

We will come back to this, but first we'll look at some cases.

In **Smith1959**, a soldier stabbed in a fight was dropped twice on the way to the treatment centre and then left untreated for some time. Although the court recognised that this contributed to the death, they found Smith, who had stabbed him, guilty of murder. As Lord Parker LCJ put it, his act was "still an operating cause and a substantial cause" of the death. A case where D's act was *not* found to have caused the death in similar circumstances is **Jordan 1956**. Here the stab wounds were healing well, but the doctor gave the victim treatment which caused an allergic reaction from which he died. The doctor's act was found to have broken the chain of causation.

The main issue is not how negligent the medical treatment is, but whether D's original act is still having an effect. It was in **Smith** but not **Jordan**, as in the latter case the original wound had almost healed so D's act was no longer a significant cause of the death. This is shown clearly in the next case.

Key case

In **Cheshire 1991**, due to negligent treatment by the hospital, complications arose after an operation on the victim of a shooting. The victim subsequently died. The person accused of the murder argued that his act had not caused the death of the victim, the hospital had done so. The court rejected the argument, following **Smith**. They said that the jury should not regard hospital treatment as excluding D's responsibility unless it "was so **independent of his acts**, and in itself so **potent in causing death**, that they regard the contribution made by his acts as insignificant."

Principle: as long as D's action was a "significant and operative" cause of the death it need not be the sole cause.

This principle was followed by the CA in **Mellor 1996**. An elderly man was taken to hospital following an attack in which he suffered broken ribs and other injuries. He died from bronchial-pneumonia brought on by his injuries. The hospital had failed to give him oxygen which may have saved him, but D was found guilty.

These cases show that the courts are reluctant to allow medical treatment to break the chain of causation and thus prevent D being found guilty.

In **Pagett 1983**, D armed himself with a shotgun and took a pregnant girl hostage in a flat. Armed police called on him to come out. He eventually did so, holding the girl in front of him as a human shield. He then fired the shotgun at the police officers who returned fire, killing the girl hostage. The actions of the police did not break the chain because shooting back at D was held to be a 'natural consequence' of his having shot first. D was convicted of manslaughter.

So causation may be proved against D even though a third person was the immediate cause. In **Chua 2015**, D worked in a hospital and had contaminated saline bags with insulin. The bags were actually administered by other nurses, but this did not break the chain of causation between his actions and the subsequent deaths caused by the contaminated bags. His actions were the significant cause of death.

In some cases D may argue that the act of the victim has broken the chain.

Key Case

In **Roberts 1971**, D – in a moving car – committed an assault on a girl by trying to take off her coat. She jumped out and was injured. He was charged with actual bodily harm. The court had to decide whether the assault caused the injury, or whether her actions broke the chain of causation. It was held that only if it was something that no reasonable person could foresee would the chain of causation be broken by the victim's actions. Here this was not the case so he was liable for her injuries. This means a judge, magistrate or jury may take into account that the victim may do the wrong thing on the spur of the moment.

Principle: If the victim's act is foreseeable it will not break the chain of causation.

To help to remember this, think of an imaginary conversation between the girl, the defendant (D) and the judge.

D: It wasn't my fault she was injured, the stupid girl jumped out of the car.

The girl: I only jumped out because I was scared you were going to hurt me.

Judge: Quite right too, a reasonable reaction and quite foreseeable in the circumstances.

It was recognised in **Roberts** that the victim might do the wrong thing in the agony of the moment. In **Williams & Davis 1992** the CA said that only if V does something "so daft or unexpected" that no reasonable person could be expected to foresee it, would the chain of causation be broken. In **Corbett 1996**, the victim was trying to escape an attack by D, when he fell and was hit by a car. V died so it was a homicide case, but the same principle applies. His action came within a foreseeable range of consequences so did not break the chain.

18

Before looking at the final rule on causation, what did you decide in Task 5? Remember legal causation turns on how significant a contribution the attack made and whether the 'intervening act' (the car, the hospital treatment or the lightning) was foreseeable. You can therefore ask:

Whether it is foreseeable that a car will come along and hit her – yes, she is lying in the road. The chain is not broken by the car.

Whether it is foreseeable that hospital treatment may be inappropriate – yes, it happens enough for it to be foreseeable. The chain is not broken by the hospital treatment.

Whether it is foreseeable that she is struck by lightning – not likely; it is very rare. In addition, as she was only slightly injured, the attack did not make a significant contribution. The chain is broken by the lightning.

Note that in the last one this does not mean the attacker gets off. He will still be liable for the attack, but not the death.

Summary

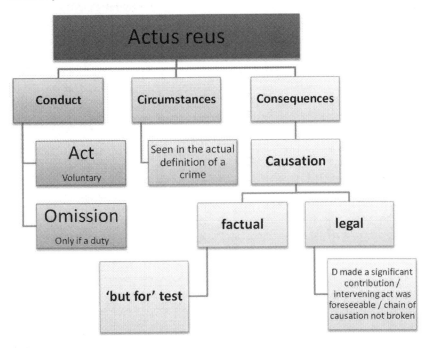

Evaluation pointer

If you were on the jury, would you know what acts should be considered 'independent' or 'potent' enough to break the causation chain? How significant is significant? What amounts to a 'daft' act by the victim? There may be a thin line between doing 'something wrong in the agony of the moment' and doing something 'daft'. This can make the decision of the jury a tough one to make.

The 'thin skull' rule

A final issue on causation is that the chain is not broken by a particular vulnerability in the victim. Lawton LJ said in **Blaue 1975**, *"those who use violence on other people must take their victims as* *they find them"*. Also known as the 'thin-skull rule', this appears to conflict with the 'foreseeability' rule. If a particular disability in the victim means that they are more likely to be harmed, or die, D is still liable even though it was not foreseeable.

Key case

In **Blaue 1975**, Lawton LJ went on to say, *"This in our judgement means the whole man, not just the physical man"*. The victim was stabbed repeatedly and rushed to hospital where doctors said she needed a blood transfusion to save her life. She was a Jehovah's Witness and so refused to have one. She consequently died. D was convicted of manslaughter; her refusal of treatment did not break the chain of causation because he had to take his victim as he found her. The 'disability' is more often physical (like a pre-existing medical condition such as a 'thin skull') but here it was the fact that she was a Jehovah's Witness.

Principle: Vulnerability in the victim does not break the chain of causation.

Examination pointer

In a problem question, look out for anything that D can argue broke the chain of causation. For example, D attacks someone and, as they are running away, they are hit by a car or bus. **Roberts** can be used to say that this is unlikely to break the chain. Look out for words like 'near the road' or 'in the bus station'. These suggest it is foreseeable. If V refuses treatment, you may need the 'thin-skull' rule. Here look out for the reason. If it is a completely idiotic decision, then **Blaue** may be distinguished. If it is due to religious beliefs, it will be followed.

Terminology

Make sure you understand the following terms:

- **Actus reus – the wrongful conduct or guilty act**
- **Omission – not acting which is not usually a crime but may be if there is a duty to act**
- **The chain of causation – the chain between D's act and the result**
- **The 'but for' test – whether the result would have occurred 'but for' D's actions**
- **The 'thin skull' rule – that some kind of vulnerability in the victim will not break the chain of causation**

Task 6

Draw a diagram like the summary above for your files. Add a case to each of the principles and keep it as a revision guide.

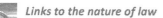 *Links to the nature of law*

Consider how far people should be liable for an omission. There is arguably a moral duty to act but it is more debatable whether there should be a legal one. You can use most of these cases to illustrate a discussion of justice, e.g., to consider whether the rules on causation achieve justice.

Self-test questions

1. *What '3 Cs' may be included in the actus reus of a crime?*
2. *On what basis did the court find liability in **Fagan**?*

3.   *Give two examples of when an omission can result in criminal liability.*

4.   *What is the thin skull rule?*

5.   *From which case did the quote at the beginning of this Chapter come?*

Answers to tasks and self-test questions are on my website at **www.drsr.org/publications/tasks.** For some interactive exercises, click on 'Free Exercises'.

*"I attach great importance to the search for a direction which is both clear and simple … I think that the **Nedrick** direction fulfils this requirement admirably." Lord Hope*

By the end of this Chapter, you should be able to:

- **Explain the term *mens rea***

- **Explain how the law on *mens rea* applies in practice**

- **Identify possible criticisms for an evaluation of the law**

Mens rea basically means a guilty mind and refers to the state of mind of the accused at the time the *actus reus* is committed. Thus *mens rea* and *actus reus* must exist at the same time.

There are two **main** types of *mens rea*. These are:

- **Intentlon**

- **Recklessness**

Other types of *mens rea* can be seen in particular offences. **Dishonesty** comes into many of the property offence. **Gross negligence** is the *mens rea* for one type of manslaughter. These are dealt with later along with those crimes, but for examples refer to the previous chapter on omissions. Where there is a duty to act, and failing to act causes a death, the result is usually manslaughter.

It is important to be able to identify both the *actus reus* and the *mens rea* of each offence when answering a problem question. Each and every part of a crime has to be proved beyond reasonable doubt.

Intention

This is the highest form of *mens rea*. For some offences, e.g., theft and murder, only intention suffices. The *mens rea* of theft is the intention to deprive someone of property permanently. If it can be shown that the property was taken absent-mindedly, D can argue that there was no *mens rea*.

Example

You borrow your friend's mobile 'phone because you have run out of credit. You forget to give it back. You have no *mens rea* so are not guilty of theft. If you borrowed it, took it home and put your own SIM card into it, this would be evidence that you intended to deprive your friend of it permanently. In these circumstances, you could be guilty of theft. Think of your own example and make a note now.

A case example is **Madeley 1990**. The host of the *Richard and Judy* television show was charged with shoplifting. He was able to show that he was suffering from stress and merely forgot to pay for the goods. The court accepted his argument and found him not guilty.

Other offences, including most of the non-fatal offences, can be committed either intentionally or recklessly. You need to know both types of *mens rea* because one of the non-fatal offences is 'wounding with intent' and this needs proof of intention; recklessness is not enough.

Although intention is the *mens rea* for 'wounding with intent' many cases you'll see here dealing with intention are homicide cases. This is because it is essentially the *mens rea* that differentiates murder from manslaughter. It is only murder if the killing is intentional. Intention can be direct or oblique (indirect). As with causation, a principle for one offence can be applied to others.

Direct Intent

Direct intent is where the result is D's aim or purpose. This is what most of us would understand by intention. If you pick up a loaded gun and fire it at someone with the aim of killing them, it can be said without any difficulty that you intended to do so. Intention was defined in **Mohan 1975** as "the decision to bring about" the result, or prohibited consequence, whether that result was desired or not. The courts have given the concept of intention a wider meaning, however. This is referred to as oblique, or indirect, intent.

Oblique intent

The consequence isn't your aim but is 'virtually certain' to occur as a result of your actions.

Example

One night, two animal rights activists set fire to a shop which sells fur coats. The shop is closed but a security guard dies in the fire. Are they guilty of murder? They do not have the *mens rea* of *direct* intent, as their purpose is to make a political point, not to kill. They may have *oblique* intent. This will depend on the evidence. We will come back to this. For now, just make a note of what you think.

The issue of intent has been problematic. **S 8 Criminal Justice Act 1967** provides that the jury *"shall not be bound in law to infer that D intended or foresaw a result of his actions by reason only of its being a natural and probable consequence of those actions"*. It also requires the jury to refer to *"all the evidence, drawing such inferences from the evidence as appear proper in the circumstances"*.

Example

Don fires a gun. The bullet kills someone. So, according to **s 8** what does the jury have to do?

The first bit means that just because it's likely to happen, it does not mean that the jury should infer that D intended it to happen. If Don fired into a crowded room, the jury may think death is a likely result, but this is *not enough by itself* to *prove* that Don intended it.

The second bit means that the jury must look at everything else. Where did it happen? What time of day was it? Did Don know there were people about? This will help the jury to decide what Don 'intended'. There is a difference between firing a gun into the air in the middle of an empty field and doing the same thing in a schoolroom. Even in the latter case, it may be that the school is closed and Don is the caretaker shooting at a rat not realising anyone is about. There is no answer which will always be right. That's what juries are for.

There has been a long line of cases on intent. Words like 'foreseeable', 'probable', 'likely' and 'natural' have all been used along the way. In **DPP v Smith 1960**, the HL had said that whether a result was probable was an objective test (what the reasonable person would "contemplate as the natural and probable result"). **S 8** makes the test subjective, whether the *defendant* saw it as probable. In **Hyam v DPP 1975**, a woman poured petrol through the letterbox of a rival and set fire to it. Two children died. She argued that she had only intended to frighten the other woman. The HL rejected her appeal but made clear the test was subjective. It was whether *she* saw the result as 'highly probable'. However, they also suggested that this was proof of intent, not just evidence of it. This point was rejected in **Moloney 1985**. It is now only a matter of evidence, not proof in itself.

In **Moloney**, D and his stepfather were having a drunken competition to see who could load and draw a shotgun the quickest. D won, and his stepfather said "I didn't think you've got the guts, but if you have, pull the trigger." D said he didn't aim the gun but just pulled the trigger. His murder conviction was quashed. The judge had directed the jury that they could find intent if D foresaw the result as 'probable' and the HL said that this was not enough; it needed to be a certainty. Lord Bridge gave an explanation of intent in terms of 'moral certainty'. However, in his later summing up he said that a consequence was 'virtually certain' if it was a 'natural consequence' (and with no mention of the word probable as required by **s 8**). This is not the same thing at all. Many 'natural' consequences are far from certain. Death from a lightning strike is a natural consequence of a storm, but not very likely – let alone certain!

In **Hancock and Shankland 1986**, two striking miners had pushed concrete blocks off a bridge to prevent a miner going to work. They said they only intended to scare him, but the driver of the taxi in which he was travelling was killed. Their conviction for murder was quashed. Both the CA and HL held that 'natural consequence' was misleading and that even awareness of the consequence as 'virtually certain' was only evidence and not proof of intent.

The law on oblique intent was clarified somewhat by the HL in **Woollin 1998**, which confirmed the direction given by the CA in **Nedrick 1986**.

The two key cases: Nedrick 1986 and Woollin 1998

In **Nedrick**, D poured paraffin through V's letterbox, circumstances not unlike those in **Hyam**, and set it alight. He said he only intended to scare her, but her child died in the resulting fire. He was convicted of murder and appealed based on lack of *mens rea*. The CA quashed his conviction because the jury had not been properly directed on intent. A conviction for manslaughter was substituted. In relation to oblique intent in a murder trial, the CA provided the following standard direction for the jury. Lord Lane said,

> *"The jury should be directed that they are not entitled to infer the necessary intention unless they feel sure that death or serious bodily harm was a **virtual certainty** (barring some unforeseen intervention) as a result of the defendant's actions and that **the defendant appreciated** that such was the case ... The decision is one for the jury to be reached on a consideration of all the evidence."*

The opening quote comes from the HL in **Woollin**. A father was convicted of murder after throwing his baby son across the room in a fit of temper. He argued that he had thrown the baby towards his pram but had not intended to kill him. His conviction was again substituted for one of manslaughter, this time by the HL. They confirmed the **Nedrick** direction.

Principle: The two questions the jury must consider as evidence of intent are:

+ was death or serious bodily harm a virtual certainty?

+ did the defendant appreciate that such was the case?

If the answer to both these questions is 'yes' then the jury may find intent. Although the HL used the word 'find' instead of 'infer', this seems of little import.

One other point. In some appeal cases, you may feel that the jury would have found intent. You could well be right. Many appeals are allowed because the jury was misdirected, not necessarily because intent could not be proved. The jury may have found sufficient evidence of intent, but were not directed correctly on the law.

Back to our example

If the defence can show that the two activists thought the shop was empty then the jury is unlikely to be convinced they appreciated that anyone's death or serious injury was a virtual certainty. They could be convicted of manslaughter but not murder. If the prosecution can prove that they knew there was a guard on duty this will be evidence for the jury that they did appreciate that death or serious injury was a virtual certainty, so a conviction for murder is possible.

I have made both **Nedrick** and **Woollin** 'Key cases' because the law was *established* by the CA in **Nedrick**, but *confirmed* by the HL in **Woollin**. A precedent carries greater weight once the HL has approved it. In addition, the **Nedrick** test has not been followed consistently. In **Walker and Hayles 1990**, although the CA held the test to be correct, they said that the use of the phrase 'a very high degree of probability' sufficed. More confusion! In **Woollin** itself, there was some confusion in the CA as to the application of the test (perhaps caused by the **Walker** decision). The Law Commission produced a report and **Draft Code**, in which it gave a definition of intent, between the cases of **Nedrick** and **Woollin**. There was therefore some doubt as to whether, if a case reached the HL, the LC's definition would be preferred to the **Nedrick** one. Apparently not.

Evaluation pointer: Intention

The **Draft Code** definition is that D acts intentionally with respect to a result *"when he acts either in order to bring it about or being aware that it will occur in the ordinary course of events"*. In **Woollin**, Lord Steyn referred to the **Draft Code** but thought the **Nedrick** test was "very similar". It is arguable that the HL should have adopted this if they thought it so similar. It seems quite clear and would become the law if the **Code** were ever adopted.

The test was followed again in **Matthews and Alleyne 2003**.

Key case

In **Matthews and Alleyne**, the Ds had thrown V from a bridge into a river. He drowned. There was evidence that he had told them he couldn't swim. They appealed against their conviction for murder. The CA rejected their appeal but again said that foresight of death as a virtual certainty does not automatically prove intent, it is merely evidence (often very strong evidence) for the jury. I have made this a key case because, unlike **Nedrick** and **Woollin**, the murder conviction was upheld by the CA.

In **Stringer 2008**, D appealed against his convictions for both murder and arson with intent to endanger life. A fire had been started at the bottom of the stairs in his house, where several of his family were sleeping. His brother died. He had denied starting the fire. At the time he was 14 and had a low IQ. The CA accepted that when directing the jury on the question of intent based on **Woollin**, the judge did not make clear the distinction between the two parts of the test (the inevitability of death or injury, and D's appreciation of it). However, on the facts, there could be only one answer to the question whether it was a virtual certainty that somebody would suffer death or serious injury from a fire in these circumstances. As to the second part of the test, even taking account of his age and low IQ the judge said that,

> "the inference that he must have appreciated it on that morning was also overwhelming. The jury's conclusion that [he] had the necessary intent was bound to follow".

So firstly, death or serious injury was a virtual certainty, and secondly, he appreciated that this was the case. He therefore had indirect intent. These are murder cases but the same principle applies to the non-fatal offences, in particular assault occasioning actual bodily harm. The only difference is that instead of serious injury or death being a virtual certainty, it will be a question of whether the assault or battery was a virtual certainty.

Examination pointer

When applying the law on intent you need only use **Nedrick** and **Woollin**, and only then in cases of oblique intent, not where it is direct. This was made clear in **Woollin**. D's knowledge will be an important factor. Look carefully at the facts for information such as 'they knew that ...' or 'unknown to them ...'. These comments will help you to apply the test as in my example. Secondly, if the offence can be committed recklessly you don't need to discuss intent at all. You can say that recklessness (see next) is enough and go on to apply the rules on that.

Summary of the development of the law on intent

Case	Development	Probable, possible or certain?	Objective / subjective Proof or evidence
DPP v Smith 1960	HL held that the *mens rea* for murder is intention to kill or cause grievous bodily harm	Foresight of death or serious injury as a natural and probable result	Objective (what the 'reasonable man or woman' would contemplate)
Hyam 1974 (similar facts to Nedrick)	Changed to a subjective test by HL	Foresight of death or serious injury as highly probable	Noted that s8 had amended this to subjective It proved intent (this seems to contradict s8 which refers to evidence)
Moloney 1985	HL disapproved **Hyam** Foreseeing death as 'probable' was not proof of intent	Foresight of death or serious injury as a moral certainty or natural consequence	Foresight was *evidence* of intent rather than *proof* of intent
Hancock and Shankland 1986	**Moloney** guidelines were followed but HL held that 'natural consequence' was misleading	The greater the probability the more likely it was foreseen and thus intended	Evidence
Nedrick 1986	CA provided a new test	Death or serious injury was a virtual certainty and D appreciated this	Evidence from which the jury can 'infer' intent
Walker and Hayles 1990	CA followed **Nedrick** but added	very high degree of probability sufficed	Evidence from which the jury can 'infer' intent
Woollin 1998	HL confirmed **Nedrick** test	Death or serious injury was a virtual certainty and D appreciated this	Evidence from which jury can 'find' intent
Matthews and Alleyne 2003 / Stringer 2008	Applied **Nedrick** test	Death or serious injury was a virtual certainty and D appreciated this	Evidence of intent is not proof of intent

Recklessness

There were two types of recklessness. Subjective recklessness is used for most crimes as an alternative *mens rea* to intent. Objective recklessness was used for criminal damage until 2003, but is now abolished. Subjective means looking at what was in the *defendant's* mind. Objective means looking at what the *reasonable person* would think. Although this no longer applies, you need to know a little about it for possible use in an extended writing question on the developments.

Cunningham 1957 provides the test for subjective recklessness. D ripped a gas meter from a basement wall in order to steal the money in the meter. Gas escaped and seeped through to an adjoining property where an occupant was overcome by the fumes. D was charged with maliciously administering a noxious substance, and argued that he did not realise the risk of gas escaping. The CA quashed his conviction having interpreted 'maliciously' to mean with subjective recklessness. The prosecution had failed to prove that D was aware that his actions might cause harm.

Principle: The test for subjective recklessness is that:

D is aware of the existence of a risk (of the consequence occurring) and deliberately goes ahead and takes that risk.

Objective recklessness was defined in **Caldwell 1982**. D, whilst drunk, set fire to a chair in the basement of the hotel where he worked. He was charged with arson (a type of criminal damage) endangering life. He argued that in his drunken state he had not thought about the fact that there could be people in the hotel. In the HL Lord Diplock extended the meaning of recklessness to include the situation where either

D saw a risk and ignored it (as in Cunningham, subjective recklessness) *or*

D gave no thought to a risk which was obvious to a reasonable person (a new meaning, objective recklessness)

In **Gemmell and Richards 2003**, the HL confirmed that recklessness is subjective and that the **Caldwell** test was wrong. Overruling its previous decision in **Caldwell**, the HL said that the *defendant* had to have recognised that there was some kind of risk.

Key case

In **Gemmell and Richards 2003**, two boys aged 11 and 13 set light to some papers outside the back of a shop. Several premises were badly damaged. They were convicted of arson on the basis of **Caldwell**, i.e., that the risk of damage was obvious to a reasonable person (in other words, objective recklessness). Their ages were therefore not taken into account. They appealed. The CA cannot overrule a decision of the HL and D's argument under the Human Rights Act also failed. They appealed further to the HL, which used the **1966 Practice Statement** to overrule its previous decision and quash the conviction.

Principle: The *mens rea* for criminal damage is now subjective (**Cunningham**) recklessness.

Thus, to prove recklessness it must be shown that *D is aware of a risk, but deliberately goes ahead and takes it.*

Evaluation pointer

Consider whether **Caldwell** or **Gemmell** is to be preferred. The latter seems to ensure greater fairness as it means D must recognise the risk of the result and if so then that shows a level of fault which should rightly be punished. However, **Caldwell** can be supported on the basis that being drunk shouldn't mean you get away with a crime. There were other cases that followed it which are harder to justify though.

In **Elliott 1983**, a 14-year old girl, who was in a special-needs class at school, set fire to a shed not realising the risk of lighting white spirit. The magistrates acquitted her. However, the prosecution successfully appealed on the basis of **Caldwell**. A reasonable person would have seen the risk that she took, so she had sufficient *mens rea*. This case shows the difficulties of applying the objective test to a child, or a person who lacks the capacity of a 'reasonable person'. However, **Gemmell** solves this problem.

Examination pointer

For a problem question involving recklessness, you only need to discuss subjective (**Cunningham**) recklessness. This is now the law as stated by the HL in **Gemmell**. A second point is that you do not need to discuss intent where the offence allows for a *mens rea* of recklessness, intent is hard to prove and unnecessary in such cases.

Task 7 (there is no answer guide for this)

Draw up a diagram with three columns. Use the first to list out all the key cases you have seen so far, use the second column for the facts and the third for the principle. Keep the diagram as a guide for revision. It might look nice on the bedroom wall.

Transferred Malice

Mens rea can be transferred from the intended victim to the actual victim. This means that if you intend to hit Steve but miss and hit Joe you cannot say "but I didn't intend to hit Joe so I had no *mens rea*". In **Latimer 1886**, D aimed a blow at X with his belt but missed and seriously wounded V. He had the intent (*mens rea*) to hit X, and this intent was transferred to the wounding (*actus reus*) of V. Thus, he had both the *mens rea* and the *actus reus* of wounding. Although usually referred to as 'transferred intent' it applies to *mens rea* generally, to both intention and recklessness. The *actus reus* and *mens rea* must be for the *same* crime.

Example

I throw a brick at someone but it misses and breaks a window. I had *mens rea* for an assault and *actus reus* for criminal damage. This *mens rea* can't be transferred. I am not guilty of either crime. If I throw the brick at someone but it hits someone else then this *mens rea* can be transferred. I had *mens rea* and *actus reus* for the *same* offence.

Coincidence of actus reus and mens rea

We saw in **Fagan v Metropolitan Police Commissioner 1969** that *actus reus* and *mens rea* must coincide, but that the court may view the *actus reus* as **continuing**. A similar reasoning can be seen in **Thabo Meli 1954**. Planning to kill him, the Ds attacked a man and then rolled what they thought was his dead body over a cliff, to make it look like an accident. He was only unconscious at this point, and the actual cause of death was exposure. The Ds were convicted of murder and argued that there were two separate acts. The first act (the attack) was accompanied by *mens rea* but was not the cause of death (so no *actus reus*). The second act (pushing him over the cliff) was the cause of death, but was not accompanied by *mens rea*. The *mens rea* of murder is intention to kill or seriously injure. They said there could be no such intention if they thought that the man was already dead. The court said that it was "impossible to divide up what was really one **series of acts**" in this way", and refused their appeal.

Make sure you understand the following terms:

- *Mens rea* – the 'guilty mind', which can be intent or subjective recklessness
- Intention – D's aim or purpose (direct intent) or knowledge that the result was a virtual certainty (indirect intent)
- Subjective recklessness – where D sees a risk but goes ahead and takes it
- Transferred malice –the *mens rea* can be transferred from the intended V to the actual V
- Coincidence of *actus reus* and *mens rea* – also called the contemporaneity rule. It means that *actus reus* and *mens rea* must exist at the same time

Summary

Level of *mens rea*	Explanation	Cases	Example crimes
• Direct Intention	• D's aim or purpose, a decision to bring about the result	• Mohan 1975	• Murder, theft, grievous bodily harm and wounding with intent
• Indirect Intention	• Result is a virtual certainty and D appreciates this	• Nedrick 1986 CA • Woollin 1998 HL	• Murder, theft, grievous bodily harm and wounding with intent
• Subjective Recklessness	• D recognises a risk and goes on to take it	• Cunningham 1957	• All other assaults, criminal damage

Links to the nature of law

In **Gemmell and Richards 2003**, where the HL used the 1966 Practice Statement to change the law on recklessness in order to achieve justice. It can also be said to be morally wrong to make a person liable when they are not aware of a risk, as in **Elliott**.

Self-test questions

1. From which case did the quote at the beginning of this Chapter come?

2. What are the two types of intent?

3. What is the **Nedrick** test for oblique intent?

4. Is recklessness now a subjective or objective test and in which case was this decided?

5. What is the principle in **Latimer**?

Answers to tasks and self-test questions are on my website at **www.drsr.org/publications/tasks.** For some interactive exercises, click on 'Free Exercises'.

Chapter 4 Strict liability

"... there has for centuries been a presumption that Parliament did not intend to make criminals of persons who were in no way blameworthy in what they did. That means that whenever a section is silent as to mens rea there is a presumption that, in order to give effect to the will of Parliament, we must read in words appropriate to require mens rea" Lord Reid

By the end of this Chapter, you should be able to:

■ **Explain the rules on strict liability**

■ **Show how the law has developed by reference to cases**

■ **Identify the arguments for and against strict liability, in order to attempt an evaluation**

As we have seen, most crimes require both *mens rea* and *actus reus.* Thus, even if D has carried out a criminal act, there will usually be no liability unless it happened with *mens rea*, in the sense of fault or blameworthiness. However, some crimes do not require *mens rea* in any form. These are called **strict liability** crimes. In these crimes, only the *actus reus* must be proved.

Some crimes do not require either *actus reus* or *mens rea*. Crimes which involve a 'state of affairs' can be committed without any apparent voluntary act by D. This is called absolute liability. It does not occur often so we will deal with it briefly first then look at strict liability in more detail.

As we saw, *actus reus* must be voluntary, so it is a defence if the offence was not committed voluntarily. In **Leicester v Pearson 1952**, the driver was acquitted of failing to give precedence to a pedestrian on a zebra crossing because his car had been pushed onto it by another car hitting him from behind. However, there are exceptions here too. Crimes of **absolute liability** arise where there is no defence to D's action.

Absolute liability: State of affairs crimes

As we saw in Chapter 2, a few crimes can be committed without any apparent voluntary act by the accused. In **Larsonneur 1933**, a Frenchwoman was deported against her will from Ireland and brought to England by the police. She was convicted under the **Aliens Order 1920** of being found in the UK without permission. The state of affairs amounting to the *actus reus* was 'being found', so as soon as she landed in the UK without the required permission she committed the offence, even though she had no choice. This particular law has since been repealed but a similar situation is seen in **Winzar v Chief Constable of Kent 1983**. A drunk was told to leave a hospital and didn't. He was removed by the police who put him in their car, which was parked on the highway. The police then arrested him for being found drunk on the highway, for which he was later convicted. As in **Larsonneur 1933**, the state of 'being found' in the circumstances was enough. So, we can see that 'state of affairs' crimes can occur where something which is normally legal may not be so in certain circumstances. Being drunk is legal, but being drunk 'on the highway' or drunk 'in charge of a motor vehicle', (a state of affairs) is not.

Statutory nature of strict liability

Strict liability most often applies to regulatory offences, i.e., offences that are not truly criminal in nature, such as traffic offences and offences covering areas of social concern or public health, such as the sale of food and alcohol, pollution and protection of the environment. These offences are usually governed by statute and the statute regulates how people must behave in certain circumstances. The statute will impose certain requirements on the relevant people and if these requirements are not satisfied, an offence will be committed. The **Health and Safety at Work Act 1974** is a good example. It imposes requirements on an employer to ensure a safe environment, competent staff and safe equipment. Other statutes cover trading standards and the sale of goods. Although these statutes are often seen as dealing with civil issues, because the person affected can sue for damages, they also create criminal offences. An employer or shopkeeper can be prosecuted as well as sued.

Example

In **Meah v Roberts 1977,** two children were served lemonade that had caustic soda in it. D was not responsible for it being there, but was found guilty under the **Food and Drug Act 1955**, even though not at fault herself because it had got into the bottle by accident.

Even though most such crimes are statutory, the courts must interpret the statutes, so case law is still important, especially if the Act is not clear on whether the offence requires *mens rea* or is a strict liability offence.

Interpretation by the courts

In **Harrow LBC v Shah 1999**, a newsagent was convicted for selling a lottery ticket to a person under 16 even though the staff had been told to ask for proof of age if there was any doubt, and the member of staff who actually sold the ticket believed the boy was over 16. It was held that the offence under the **National Lottery Regulations 1994** was one of strict liability, so there was no need to prove an intent, or even recklessness, as regards the age of the buyer of the ticket. The act of selling it to someone under 16 was enough.

Some statutes specifically provide a defence to strict liability crimes where D can prove that all due care was taken. This is known as the 'due diligence' defence. An example is the **Licensing Act 2003** which provides a defence to various offences under the **Act**, such as selling alcohol to young people, if D "exercised all due diligence to avoid committing the offence".

However, the courts have been reluctant to develop this approach so it only applies where the statute specifically allows for it. Thus the court found the newsagent guilty in **Shah**, even though he had taken care, as the **National Lottery Regulations** had no such provision. The Law Commission (in their 2010 report on the issue) has suggested that the due diligence defence should apply in all cases.

In **Smedley's v Breed 1974**, a caterpillar was found in a can of peas. Although the manufacturers had supplied millions of cans of peas (all without caterpillars!) they were convicted, as in **Meah v Roberts**, under the **Food and Drug Act 1955** for selling food that was unfit for human consumption.

Most strict liability crimes are fairly minor, and not usually seen as truly criminal. Someone convicted may have broken the law but there is little social stigma attached to the act, even though illegal. In 'real' crimes there is more controversy about finding someone guilty without fault, and this can be seen in **Sweet v Parsley 1970**.

Key case

In **Sweet v Parsley**, a woman let rooms to students. The police raided the premises and found cannabis. She was charged with being *"concerned in the management of premises used for the purpose of smoking cannabis"* under the **Dangerous Drugs Act 1965**. She was found guilty even though not at fault – she was completely unaware of the cannabis smoking. The HL eventually acquitted her and established the rule that strict liability could only be imposed where the Act specifically made the offence one of strict liability. In all other cases, a need for *mens rea* would be presumed.

Principle: If the Act is silent on the issue of *mens rea*, it will be interpreted so that D must either intend or be reckless regarding the criminal act.

In **K 2001,** D (who was aged 26) had sexual activity with a girl of 14 and was charged with indecent assault. He said he believed she was over 16. The HL accepted that he did not have *mens rea* and said the offence was not one of strict liability, so he was not guilty. This case indicated that the old case of **Prince 1875**, where D had been convicted of taking a girl under the age of 16 out of the possession of her parents, was wrong. She had told him she was 18 and, as she looked much older than she actually was, he believed her. D was convicted even though he had acted without *mens rea*. Lord Steyn described the decision in **Prince** as "a relic from an age dead and gone". The HL confirmed that, as stated in **Sweet v Parsley**, there was an overriding presumption of statutory interpretation that *mens rea* was needed unless there were express indications to the contrary in the statute. The presumption of *mens rea* is particularly strong in serious offences.

However in **G 2008**, in similar circumstances, a conviction was upheld. Here the charge was rape. A boy of fifteen had sexual intercourse with a girl of 12 without her consent but believing her to be 15. He was charged with rape of a child under 13 and the CA upheld his conviction on the basis that Parliament clearly intended the offence to be one of strict liability as regards age. There was a defence available where the child was over 13 and the fact that this was in the Act made it clear that the defence *only* applied in the case of older children.

In **Taylor 2016**, D took a car without consent and collided with a scooter. The scooter rider later died and D was charged with aggravated vehicle taking (**Theft Act s 12A**) and with causing a death while uninsured (**Road Traffic Act 1988**). As regards causing a death while uninsured, the prosecution had accepted that the decision in **Hughes 2013** applied, where the SC had held that there must be some element of fault in the driving which contributed to the death, so D was found not guilty under the RTA. He was convicted under the **Theft Act** and appealed. Aggravated vehicle taking includes taking a vehicle and then either driving dangerously or causing injury 'owing to the driving'. The prosecution argued that *mens rea* was only needed as regards the taking of the vehicle and nothing more. The SC held that having *mens rea* for the first offence could not equate to having it for the more serious offence of causing the death. The SC pointed out that this was not a regulatory offence, referring to **Sweet v Parsley**. Lord Sumption said that there must be some element of fault in the driving which contributed to the death. Here there was no evidence that D was driving dangerously and the fact that he had taken the car without consent was not enough; that did not cause the death.

social utility (usefulness) and public policy

One of the main reasons for imposing strict liability is that it is beneficial to society as a whole because it makes people more careful and protects people from harm. An example is **Meah v Roberts** above. Thus, offences covering areas of social concern such as the sale of food and drink, pollution and the protection of the environment are strict liability offences and this can be justified by the nature of the offence. The decision in **Shah** could be justified on the basis that underage gambling is a matter of social concern.

In **Alphacell v Woodward 1972**, the HL held that the offence of causing polluted matter to enter a river was a strict liability offence because pollution was a matter of the "utmost public importance".

The rules on strict liability were set out in **Gammon (Hong Kong) Ltd v AG of HK 1985**.

Key case

In **Gammon**, builders were held liable for carrying out building works in a way likely to cause damage, where they had not followed the original plans exactly. Safety regulations had prohibited 'substantial changes' and the builders argued that they hadn't known the changes they made *were* substantial. The offence was said to be one of strict liability because it was aimed at protecting public safety. In this case Lord Scarman laid down guidelines for the courts when considering whether an offence was one of strict liability. These include:

there is a presumption that *mens rea* is required

it is particularly strong if the offence is 'truly' criminal

it can only be displaced if the statute clearly states or implies this (e.g., with words such as 'knowingly' or 'maliciously')

it can only be displaced if the statute deals with an issue of social concern and public safety is an issue

A related issue to social utility is that of public policy. This means a government policy that provides a law for the well-being of society as a whole. The last point in **Gammon** is based on policy. It would be against public policy for people to be unsafe. Therefore, any law involving safety is more likely to be accepted by the courts as a strict liability offence.

The approach in **Gammon** was followed in **Blake 1997**. D was a disc jockey who was convicted under the **Wireless Telegraphy Act 1949** for broadcasting without a licence. D was in his flat at the time of the broadcast and argued that he thought he was making tapes and not transmitting. The CA felt that as unlicensed transmissions could interfere with the emergency services and air traffic control, the issue was one of public safety. On this basis, the offence could be classed as one of strict liability.

In **Jackson 2006**, the CA held that flying an aircraft at a height lower that 100 feet was a strict liability offence under the **Air Force Act 1955**. The Judge referred to both **Sweet v Parsley** and **Gammon** and ruled that there was no wording in the **Air Force Act** which required proof that D knew that he was flying below the permitted height. This meant the statute created an offence of strict liability. D's argument that the prosecution needed to prove at least recklessness was rejected. The creation of the offence was to protect the public and the public interest overrode the need to prove *mens rea*.

Examination pointer

In a question on strict liability you should not only be able to discuss what it is and when it applies, but also to provide an evaluation. There are several arguments for and against imposing strict liability and the following section will give you some ideas. Try to develop your own arguments too; you will sound more confident if you do. Also remember that liability is usually based on blameworthiness, or fault and that strict liability is an exception to this.

Arguments for and against imposing strict liability

There is never going to be a right answer as to whether the imposition of strict liability is a good thing or not. There will be valid arguments on both sides and views may change depending on the circumstances.

Example

It has been snowing and there are piles of snow at the side of the road. I manage to park my car and go shopping. When I come back, I have a parking ticket. It turns out I have parked on a double yellow line, but I couldn't see it. It would be very hard to prove I *knew* I had parked on a yellow line in the snow, so had *mens rea*. It would take up a lot of court time for what is only a minor matter. It can therefore be argued that strict liability is right as a small fine can be issued without a waste of time and taxpayers' money. On the other hand, it seems unfair because I did not know I was doing anything wrong because I could not see the yellow lines. There will be people on both sides of this argument and no-one will be either right or wrong.

The Law Commission suggested in a 2010 report that Parliament should state more clearly whether an offence was one of strict liability or not, which seems a sensible way forward but has not yet been seen in practice.

Arguments against:

- it is unfair to convict D of a criminal offence without proving *mens rea*

- it leads to the punishment of people who have taken all possible precautions

- it also means such people have a criminal record

- imposing a requirement of negligence would be fairer to D, but is a low level of fault so would still protect the public by making D careful

Arguments for:

- it makes people more careful

- it protects the public

- most such offences are minor and carry no social stigma

- proving *mens rea* is hard in many minor offences so time and money is saved

- **the judge can address the issue of fault when sentencing**

Examination pointer

I said that when discussing the reasons behind the concept of strict liability it is a good idea to look at it from both sides, i.e. provide a balanced argument. However, it is always important to read the question carefully – if you are only asked to discuss one or the other keep just to that.

Task 8

Choose one argument for and one against strict liability and develop them. Use a case for each to support your views and keep this for revision.

Briefly explain whether you think strict liability should, or should not, be imposed in the following situations.

- polluting the river
- jumping a traffic light
- murder
- selling food which is not fit for human consumption
- selling alcohol to a 15-year old

Summary

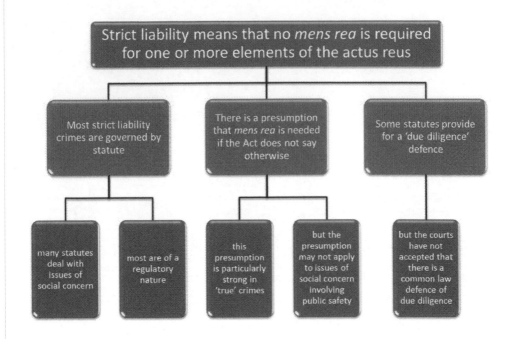

Task 9 – terminology

Make sure you understand the following terms. Add a short description to each one.

- **Strict liability**
- **Absolute liability**
- **Statutory nature**
- **Social utility**
- **Public policy**
- **Regulatory offences**

Links to the nature of law

For this area morality is relevant because it seems immoral to make someone liable where there is no evidence of fault. Justice may be achieved in regulatory crimes and society is protected by making people more careful. However, some of these cases do not serve justice especially those involving in more serious crimes like **G 2008**.

Self-test questions

1. *State three areas of social concern where strict liability applies*

2. Which case established that there is a presumption of mens rea in most criminal offences where the Act is silent on the matter?

3. In which case were the guidelines set out for imposing strict liability where the Act is silent?

4. State three reasons for imposing strict liability

5. State three reasons for not imposing strict liability

Answers to tasks and self-test questions are on my website at **www.drsr.org/publications/tasks.** For some interactive exercises, click on 'Free Exercises'.

*"There could be no dispute that if you touch a person's clothes while he is wearing them that is equivalent to touching him." **R v Thomas 1985***

By the end of this Chapter, you should be able to:

- **Explain the *actus reus* and *mens rea* of assault and battery**
- **Explain the differences between them**
- **Explain how the law applies in practice by reference to cases**
- **Identify possible criticisms for an evaluation of the law**

Common assault includes two separate offences, assault and battery. It is called common assault because it comes from the common law. This means that assault and battery are not defined in any statute so the rules come from cases. The **Criminal Justice Act 1988 s 39** classifies them as summary offences (triable only in the magistrates' court) so for convenience they are charged under this section.

Examination pointer

It is better not to say they are *offences* under **s 39 Criminal Justice Act**. They are common law offences *charged* under the **Act**. Think of common assault as an umbrella under which the two crimes of assault and battery sit. They frequently occur together. If you need to discuss both, then refer to common assault and then describe assault and battery in turn.

Assault and battery are also trespass to the person which is a civil matter, a tort. Here we are only dealing with *criminal* assault. The definitions as developed by case law are currently:

Assault: to cause someone to apprehend immediate and unlawful personal violence

Battery: the unlawful application of force to another

Example

Fred raises his fist and threatens Simon with a punch on the nose. This is an assault because Simon 'apprehends', or fears, violence. If Fred then follows up the threat there is both an assault and a battery. It may also be actual bodily harm, but we'll come to that later.

We will look at each offence in turn.

Assault

The definition of assault is "an act by which a person **intentionally or recklessly causes another to apprehend immediate and unlawful violence**". This definition was used by the CA in **Ireland 1996** (discussed below) and confirmed by the HL the following year, in the twin appeals of **Ireland & Burstow 1997**.

Actus reus

The *actus reus* is to:

- **cause the victim to apprehend**

- **immediate and unlawful violence**

Cause the victim to apprehend

Apprehend means to become aware of or look forward to. Here it is not look forward to in the positive sense but with a sense of fear. It is the effect on the victim that is important with assault. Assault is not the actual violence but the *threat* of it, so as long as V expects violence to take place, that is enough.

Example

D walks into a bank pointing a banana concealed in a bag and saying, "I have a gun. Give me the money or I'll shoot you." The cashier is very frightened and does as D says. This is an assault. The fact that there is no possibility of carrying out the threat doesn't matter. V is in fear of immediate violence.

D walks into a bank pointing a real gun and saying, "Give me the money or I'll shoot." The cashier knows him from college and she thinks he is doing it as a joke. This is unlikely to be assault. V doesn't believe that any violence is about to take place.

Whether it amounts to assault therefore depends on whether or not V *thinks* that violence is about to take place.

Can words alone constitute an assault?

Early cases indicated that words would not amount to assault unless accompanied by some threatening gesture (like raising your fist). In **Meade and Belt 1823**, it was said that "no words or singing are equivalent to an assault". This has changed over the years and in **Wilson 1955**, the words "get out the knives" was said to be enough for assault. Also in **Constanza 1997**, a case of stalking, the CA held that words alone could amount to an assault. Even silence is now capable of amounting to an assault. In **Smith v Chief Superintendent of Woking Police Station 1983**, a 'peeping Tom' assaulted a woman by looking at her through her bedroom window at night. He had caused her to be frightened.

Evaluation pointer

It is the effect on the victim that is important, thus it seems right that words – or even silence – should amount to assault if they put the victim in fear of harm. The law has arguably become more satisfactory over the years, at least on this point.

Key case

In **Ireland**, D had repeatedly made silent telephone calls, accompanied by heavy breathing, to three women who then suffered psychiatric illness. In the appeal to the HL in 1997, Lord Steyn confirmed that words would be enough for assault, saying,

> "The proposition that a gesture may amount to an assault, but that words can never suffice, is unrealistic and indefensible. A thing said is also a thing done. There is no reason why something said should be incapable of causing an apprehension of immediate personal violence, e.g., a man accosting a woman in a dark alley saying 'come with me or I will stab you.' I would, therefore, reject the proposition that an assault can never be committed by words".

Words may prevent an assault

If D accompanies the threat with words which indicate that no violence will take place then there is no assault. An example of this is seen in a very old case. In **Turbeville v Savage 1669**, D was having an argument with V and placed his hand on the hilt of his sword. This would indicate an assault. He then said "If it were not assize time, I would not take such language from you". There was held to be no assault. The statement was held to indicate that he would *not* assault V because it was assize time and the judges were in town.

Example

You say to John "I would hit you if it were not your birthday." This indicates you won't do so (assuming it is his birthday!). No assault has taken place.

immediate and unlawful violence

The threat must be of 'immediate' violence. This means if you threaten someone just as you are about to get on a train it won't be enough. You can't carry out your threat 'immediately'. The term is widely interpreted though. In **Smith v Chief Superintendent of Woking Police Station**, V was scared by D looking at her through her bedroom window at night. She was frightened of what he might do next. The CA held this was sufficient.

In **Ireland 1996**, D argued that the 'immediacy' requirement was lacking. The CA held it was satisfied because by putting himself in contact with the victims D had caused them to be in immediate fear.

Evaluation pointer

Is immediate fear the same thing as fear of immediate harm? The CA in **Ireland** seemed to think so. The appeal to the HL did not focus on this issue so it remains unclear. If D phones V and says, "I have planted a bomb in your house. It is set to go off in 5 minutes." there is no problem. Both the fear and the harm are immediate. However, if D says "I have planted a bomb in your house. It is set to go off in a week." then it is a different matter. V may be in immediate fear, but is not in fear of immediate harm.

On a positive note, the courts appear to be reacting to the reality of the times. In **Ireland**, the CA said, "*We must apply the law to the conditions as they are in the 20th century*".

It is now the 21st century and the law will hopefully be applied taking into account the latest methods of communication which are much more 'immediate'.

Note that in many of these cases some actual harm was also caused. This means they can come under the statutory offence of an assault occasioning actual bodily harm under **s 47 Offences Against the Persons Act 1861** as happened in **Roberts 1971**. They are discussed here as well as the next Chapter because for **s 47** to be satisfied an assault or battery must take place first.

Evaluation pointer

A good argument that words should suffice is that they can sometimes be just as threatening as a gesture. As in the 'bomb' example I used earlier. Also in a society that has a sophisticated communications network the immediacy issue is more easily satisfied.

Mens rea

In **Savage1991**, Lord Ackner said, "... the mental element of assault is an intention to cause the victim to apprehend unlawful and immediate violence or recklessness whether such an apprehension is caused". That recklessness for all assaults is **Cunningham** (subjective) recklessness was confirmed in the joint appeals of **Savage & Parmenter 1992**.

Applying the mens rea rules to assault

For **direct intent**, the prosecution must prove that it was D's aim or purpose to cause the victim to apprehend unlawful and immediate violence.

For **indirect intent**, it must be proved that it was a virtual certainty that V would apprehend immediate and unlawful violence and that D appreciated this.

For **recklessness**, it must be proved that D recognises a risk that V would apprehend immediate and unlawful violence but goes ahead and takes that risk.

Battery

Battery is the unlawful application of force to another. As noted earlier it often follows an assault. Assault and battery therefore go together in many, but not all, cases.

Example

In my earlier example of the punch on the nose, there would be both. Simon saw the punch coming, so he was in fear of harm. If Fred hit Simon from behind this would only be a battery. No assault would have occurred because Simon was not in fear.

Actus reus

The *actus reus* is the unlawful application of force to another. It can be slight because the law sees people's bodies as inviolate. Lane LCJ said in **Faulkner and Talbot 1981**, that it was "any intentional touching of another person without the consent of that person and without lawful excuse. It need not necessarily be hostile, or rude, or aggressive, as some earlier cases seemed to indicate".

In **Thomas 1985**, the court said, "if you touch a person's clothes whilst he is wearing them that is equivalent to touching him".

In 2011, the TV presenter Fiona Bruce was sprayed with some aerosol string while she was filming an episode of Antiques Roadshow. The Ds were charged with common assault, specifically battery, for applying unlawful force.

Unlawful

Part of the *actus reus* is that the force must be unlawful. In **Collins v Wilcock 1984**, a police constable who took hold of a woman's arm was acting unlawfully so his actions amounted to battery. If there had been a lawful arrest this would not have been the case.

Consent may make the application of force lawful. Consent may be implied, e.g., most sports contacts are not battery because there is implied consent to touching.

Consent

As well as making the battery lawful, consent is also a defence. It is therefore covered in detail in Chapter 17 because it applies to other crimes. Here we are just looking at it briefly as part of the *actus reus* of common assault (assault and battery). If consent is shown then the threat or act is not unlawful, so the *actus reus* is not complete.

Consent can be express or implied.

In **AG's Reference (No 6 of 1980) 1981**, a fight between two youths resulted in one of them suffering a bloody nose. The other was charged with assault occasioning actual bodily harm. The CA held that consent did not apply in that case (mainly because it was a fight in public), but listed some circumstances where it could. These included properly conducted games and sports, and reasonable surgical interference. In circumstances like these consent may be implied even if not expressly given.

There is implied consent to harm in most contact sports. Where D's conduct was not within the rules of the game, the position was unclear, but was clarified in **Barnes 2004**. D had injured another player during a late tackle in a football match. His conviction was quashed and the CA held that criminal cases should be reserved for times when the conduct was *"sufficiently grave to be categorised as criminal"*. It now seems that consent can make the act lawful in most sporting cases – but it would not apply if a player punched the referee for making a bad decision!

Case law has long viewed 'manly sports' and 'manly diversions' as lawful activities. In **Jones 1988**, a group of boys tossed two other boys 10 feet into the air resulting in injuries. This seems more than 'properly conducted games and sports' but it was accepted that there was implied consent to such 'rough horseplay'.

It is generally accepted that consent must be real. Thus, consent by a child or consent induced by fraud may not be valid, even if expressly given. In **Burrell and Harmer 1967**, a 12- and 13-year-old were not deemed to have consented to actual bodily harm caused by tattooing.

Self-defence also makes a battery lawful. This is also discussed further in Chapter 17 as it applies to most offences. For now just be aware that if people act in self-defence then they may have a defence against any harm caused.

Application of force

There is a requirement that force is applied. Battery cannot be caused by an omission; there must be an act. This was confirmed in **Fagan v Metropolitan Police Commissioner 1969**. D argued that not moving off the police officer's foot was an omission not an act. The court confirmed that battery could not be committed by omission, but found him guilty on the basis that there was a continuing act. The *actus reus* was the driving onto the police officer's foot and staying there.

Direct or indirect force

Some early cases suggest that the force had to be direct but this is unlikely to be the case now. In **DPP v K 1990**, a schoolboy put acid in a hot air drier. Later another pupil used the drier and was badly scarred by the acid. This was held to be a battery. The case raised another issue. The boy had been using the acid in an experiment in class and was merely trying to hide it. He did not have *mens rea* when he put it in the machine, but he did have *mens rea* when he failed to do anything about it. We saw above that a battery could not be committed by omission. In **DPP v K**, omitting to rectify what he had done was held to be enough though.

In **Haystead 2000**, the harm appeared to be indirect. Here, D punched his girlfriend who was holding her baby. She dropped the baby resulting in the baby hitting his head on the floor. The defendant was convicted of battery on the baby.

Evaluation pointer

Although in **Haystead**, it seemed to be indirect force it may just be a widening of the meaning of direct. The court held that direct could include *via* another person or a weapon. Thus setting a dog on someone can be seen as direct force. This is reasonable, as it is unlikely to be argued that throwing a brick at someone was not direct and there is little real difference.

As a recap let's have a few more examples.

Examples

Matt threatens to hit Leon, who is scared. This is an assault because Leon 'apprehends', or fears, immediate violence.

Matt threatens to hit Leon but Leon thinks he is joking. Leon is not in fear of violence so part of the *actus reus* is missing and there is no assault.

Matt threatens to hit Leon if he ever sees him in the area again. Even if Leon is in fear of violence, he is not in fear of *immediate* violence. Again, part of the *actus reus* is missing, so there is no assault.

Matt hits Leon. This is battery as Matt has used unlawful force (there is no need for any injury or harm to result).

Matt taps Leon on the shoulder to attract his attention. Even though he has applied force, it is *lawful* force, because there is implied consent to this type of touching. Part of the *actus reus* is missing, so there is no battery.

Matt threatens to hit Leon and then does so. Here there is both an assault and a battery.

Matt hits Leon from behind. Here there is a battery but no assault because Leon cannot be in fear of violence if he doesn't see it coming.

Mens rea

As with assault, the *mens rea* is intent or recklessness. The *mens rea* of battery is intent or recklessness to cause unlawful force (**Venna 1976**).

Here it is as to whether force is applied.

Task 10

Look back at the application of the rules on intent and recklessness to an assault. Apply the same rules for a case of battery.

Terminology

Make sure you understand the following terms:

- **Common assault – means an assault or a battery**
- **Apprehend – means to fear**
- **Consent – may make a battery lawful**

Summary

Assault *Actus reus*	
to cause the victim to apprehend	What is the effect on the victim?
immediate and unlawful personal violence	Ireland
Words may be enough, or even silence	Wilson/Ireland
	intent to cause the victim to apprehend immediate and
Mens rea	unlawful personal violence or being subjectively reckless as to this
Battery *Actus reus*	
unlawful application of force to another	Collins v Wilcock
Can include touching V's clothes	Thomas
May include indirect force	DPP v K
	intent to apply unlawful force
Mens rea	or being subjectively reckless as to this

Links to the nature of law

Justice requires fairness and certainty and it can be said that having offences developed only through the common law, with changing definitions, lacks certainty and clarity. This goes against both justice and the rule of law.

Self-test questions

1. What is the current definition of assault?

2. Can words alone constitute an assault? Use a case to support your answer.

3. What is the mens rea for assault?

4. Does a battery have to be hostile? Use a case to support your answer.

5. What two defences may make a battery lawful?

Answers to tasks and self-test questions are on my website at **www.drsr.org/publications/tasks.** For some interactive exercises, click on 'Free Exercises'.

"It has been recognised for many centuries that putting a person in fear may amount to an assault. The early cases predate the invention of the telephone. We must apply the law to the conditions as they are in the 20th century". Swinton L.J

By the end of this Chapter, you should be able to:

■ Explain the *actus reus* of ABH as an assault or battery which causes harm

■ Explain the *mens rea* of ABH

■ Explain how the law applies in practice by reference to cases

■ Identify possible criticisms for an evaluation of the law

This offence comes under **s 47 Offences against the Persons Act 1861**. It is commonly known as *ABH*. **S 47** provides:

*"whosoever shall be convicted on indictment of any **assault occasioning actual bodily harm** shall be liable to imprisonment for not more than five years"*

Until 1984, it was thought that the Act merely provided for a greater penalty where an assault resulted in harm being caused. It is now clear that a new offence was created (**Courtie 1984**). In fact, in **Savage1991**, Lord Ackner indicated that it created two offences, an assault occasioning ABH and a battery occasioning ABH.

The offence has the *actus reus* and *mens rea* of assault or battery plus the further *actus reus* of some harm being caused. Let's look at this in more detail.

Actus reus

There are three parts to this.

■ assault – the conduct, an assault or battery

■ occasioning – a matter of causation

■ actual bodily harm – the consequence

Assault

The offence is an *assault* occasioning actual bodily harm. Assault, as we saw, covers both assault and battery. This is seen in **Savage1991**.

Key case

In **Savage**, a girl threw a glass of beer over another girl. As she did so, she let go of the glass which broke, resulting in a cut to the other girl's wrist. The throwing of the beer was enough for a battery. Lord Ackner said, *"It is of course common ground that Mrs Savage committed an assault upon Miss Beal when she threw the contents of her glass of beer over her."* In referring to assault, he is describing a battery, confirming that the word assault in **s 47** includes both assault and battery.

There was no proof she intended to throw the glass and she said it was an accident. However, she did intend to throw the beer. The throwing of the beer was enough for the *actus reus* of battery. She intended to do this, so there was *mens rea* too. Once battery was proved, for her to be convicted under **s 47** the prosecution merely had to show this had 'occasioned' (caused) the harm.

Principle: *Mens rea* is needed only as regards the assault or battery, not the harm.

So, 'assault' for **s 47** requires the *actus reus* and *mens rea* of an assault or a battery. This will include each and every part, so, e.g., if there is consent to the battery it will be lawful and so cannot amount to ABH.

In **Wilson 1996**, a husband branded his initials on his wife's buttocks. It was done at her request but she needed medical attention and he was charged with ABH. The CA accepted that she had consented to the harm so he was not guilty.

In **R v R 1991**, a man was convicted of ABH and rape. He appealed, arguing that both the rape and the ABH were lawful. This was on the basis that although separated he was married to the woman, and there was an old common law tradition that a woman consented to sex by marrying. The CA found him guilty and the HL followed the CA's reasoning and confirmed there was no longer immunity based on consent for a man who assaulted and raped his wife

Occasioning

Occasioning means bringing about, or causing. **S 47** is a result crime so the prosecution must show that the assault or battery caused the result (actual bodily harm). D's actions must make a significant contribution to the harm and the chain of causation must not be broken.

Task 11

Look back at Chapter 2 on *actus reus* and causation. Read **Roberts** to remind you of the facts. The question was whether the battery by D caused the harm. Why did the action by the victim not break the chain of causation? What type of action might do so?

In **Savage**, the HL said that once the assault was established, the only remaining question was whether the victim's conduct was the natural consequence of that assault. According to Lord Ackner,

> *"the word 'occasioning' raised solely a question of causation, an objective question which does not involve inquiring into the accused's state of mind".*

Occasioning therefore relates to *actus reus* not *mens rea*. There is no need to intend any harm at all.

Examination pointer

Causation is a common issue in a problem question where a result crime like ABH is involved. If harm has occurred, you may need to discuss all three of these offences. You will certainly have to discuss two of them because **s 47** cannot happen without one of the others. You will need to define and explain assault and/or battery. Then define harm. Finally show that the assault (or battery) caused the harm. Use a case like **Roberts** or **Savage** to explain this and apply it to the facts given. If those facts remind you of a more relevant case, use that instead.

Finally, you will need to explain *mens rea*, but only regarding the assault. We'll come back to this.

Actual bodily harm

In **Miller 1954**, actual bodily harm was held to be any hurt or injury calculated to "interfere with health or comfort", which could include mental discomfort. In **Chan-Fook 1994**, the CA qualified this a little. Psychiatric injury was enough but not "mere emotions" such as fear, distress or panic. Really trivial or insignificant harm is excluded. Some type of identifiable medical condition will be needed, but it is clear that harm is not confined to physical injury.

In **DPP v Ross Smith 2006**, the QBD held that cutting someone's hair without consent amounted to assault occasioning actual bodily harm. At trial, the magistrates had accepted that as the victim had suffered no physical or psychological harm the offence was not proved. The QBD disagreed. Referring to **Chan-Fook** and **Burstow**, it was held that 'harm' included hurt or damage and 'actual' meant merely that it was not trivial harm. 'Bodily' harm applied to all parts of the body, of which hair was a part, and her hair had been cut so there was 'bodily harm'. The court also held that pain was not a necessary requirement of actual bodily harm.

Note that this case is actually **DPP v Smith 2006** but you will see reference to either Ross or Michael (his first two names) in most textbooks as Smith is a common name.

Key case

In **Ireland 1996**, silent 'phone calls which caused psychiatric harm came under **s 47**. D's argument was that there was no assault because there was no fear of 'immediate' harm. If there was no assault, there could be no assault occasioning actual bodily harm. The argument failed as the court found sufficient 'immediacy' in a telephone call. The CA also relied on **Chan-Fook** to confirm that psychiatric harm was enough for 'bodily harm'. The opening quote came from the CA and was approved in the HL.

Principles: Silence can amount to assault; harm includes psychiatric harm and immediacy is wide-ranging.

Mens rea

The *mens rea* is intent or recklessness.

D need not intend, or be reckless as to, any harm, only the assault or battery. This was held to be the case by the CA in **Roberts 1971**. D argued that he did not intend to cause harm and nor was he reckless. He was found guilty because he had the *mens rea* and the *actus reus* for the battery, plus harm had been caused. This was enough for **s 47**. Despite this seemingly clear principle of law, there was conflict in several cases over the next 20 years.

Key case

The issue was finally put beyond doubt by the HL in the joint appeals of **Savage & Parmenter 1992**. These two cases had been decided differently in the lower courts. The principle of **Roberts** had been followed in **Savage** but not in **Parmenter**.

In **Savage & Parmenter**, the HL held **Roberts** to be the correct law. The throwing of the beer with intent to do so was enough for a battery. The question for the court was whether a further mental state had to be established in relation to the bodily harm element of the **s 47** offence. Lord Ackner said, *"Clearly the section, by its terms, expressly imposes no such requirement"*.

This means that if D has *mens rea* for the assault and additionally harm occurs, it can amount to the more serious charge under **s 47**. Think about it as an equation:

Assault (AR + MR of assault or battery) + occasions (AR, causation) + harm (AR consequence) = **s 47**

Sandra shouts threateningly at Tara. Tara is scared that Sandra will hit her. She jumps back and hits her head causing severe bruising. This will be enough for a charge under **s 47**. There is the *actus reus* of an assault (Tara is in fear of immediate violence) plus *mens rea* (Sandra intends to frighten her) and this assault occasioned (caused – jumping back and falling is foreseeable, as in **Roberts**) actual bodily harm (severe bruising).

So, the *mens rea* for **s 47** is intent or subjective recklessness as to the assault only, not the harm. The prosecution will have to show one of the following:

- **Direct intent:** causing fear of violence or the application of force is D's aim or purpose.

- **Indirect intent:** D appreciates that it is virtually certain that the V will fear violence, or D appreciates that the application of force is virtually certain.

- **Subjective recklessness:** D is aware of the risk of V being in fear, or is aware of the risk of force being applied, and goes ahead anyway.

Terminology

Make sure you understand the following terms:

- **Occasioning – means causing**

- **Actual bodily harm – is some type of hurt that is more than trivial and can be physical or psychiatric**

Evaluation pointer

One problem with **s 47** is that the *mens rea* does not match the *actus reus*. For the *actus reus* of **s 47** you need ABH to have occurred, the *mens rea* is only for assault or battery though (**Roberts**, **Savage**). This is confusing, and arguably unfair. Should D be guilty of causing ABH where there was only intent to scare someone? On the other hand, should D get away with harming someone when the attempt to scare them caused harm?

Summary of s 47

Actus reus: Assault = assault or battery (**Savage**)

Actus reus: Occasioning = causing (the assault or battery must cause the harm **Roberts, Savage**)

Actus reus: Actual bodily harm = discomfort (**Miller**) but not trivial harm (**Chan Fook**). Includes psychiatric harm (**Ireland**)

Mens rea : Intent or recklessness as to the assault or battery (**Roberts, Savage**)

Links to the nature of law

Justice requires fairness and certainty and the lack of match between *mens rea* and *actus reus* in **s 47** is not fair. The non-fatal offences have been the subject of much criticism and proposals for reform by the Law Commission. These are covered in more detail in the summary following the next chapter as they apply to all the offences.

Self-test questions

1. From which case did the opening quote come?

2. What are the three parts to the actus reus?

3. For which part of this is mens rea needed?

4. According to **Roberts**, what sort of action by V could break the chain of causation?

5. In which case did the HL finally confirm that the principle in **Roberts** was correct?

Answers to tasks and self-test questions are on my website at **www.drsr.org/publications/tasks.** For some interactive exercises, click on 'Free Exercises'.

"*In the context of a criminal act therefore the words 'cause' and 'inflict' may be taken to be interchangeable.*" Lord Hope

By the end of this Chapter, you should be able to:

- Explain the *actus reus* of wounding and GBH in s 20 and s 18

- Explain the difference in the *mens rea* between the two sections

- Explain how the law applies in practice by reference to cases

- Identify possible criticisms and explain the proposed reforms for all the non-fatal offences

Section 20 makes it an offence to:

"*unlawfully and maliciously wound or inflict any grievous bodily harm upon any other person, either with or without any weapon or instrument*"

Section 18 makes it an offence to:

"*unlawfully and maliciously by any means whatsoever wound or cause any grievous bodily harm to any person with intent to do some grievous bodily harm to any person*"

These two offences are commonly called malicious wounding (**s 20**) and wounding with intent (**s 18**). However, there are actually two separate offences under each section.

- **unlawfully and maliciously wounding**

- **unlawfully and maliciously inflicting / causing grievous bodily harm**

There is very little difference in the *actus reus*; each needs **either** a wound **or** serious injury. We will deal with the two sections together for *actus reus* and then look at the different *mens rea* for each.

Actus reus for s 18 and s 20

There are four matters to consider.

- **unlawfully**

- **wound**

- **inflict / cause**

- **grievous bodily harm**

We'll take these in turn. I have left out 'malicious' for the moment as this has been treated as relating to *mens rea*.

Unlawfully

If the act is done lawfully, no offence has occurred. Thus if D has acted in self-defence this makes it lawful, so part of the *actus reus* is missing. Consent may also make it lawful, but is not usually applicable to serious harm, only ABH, as discussed earlier.

In **Brown 1994**, the House of Lords decided that consent of the victim could no longer be a defence if serious harm was *intended*. This can be compared with **Wilson 1996** where a man branded his initials on his wife's buttocks and it was accepted that the wife consented to ABH. In **Dica 2004**, D had consensual sex with two women knowing he was HIV positive. They both became infected with HIV and he was convicted under **s 20** with recklessly inflicting grievous bodily harm. On appeal, the CA confirmed the point in **Brown** that consent was not a defence to *intentional* harm. However, as the charge was *recklessly* inflicting grievous bodily harm, they held that the issue of consent should not have been withdrawn from the jury. A retrial was ordered at which he was found guilty under **s 20**. In **Golding 2014**, a man infected his girlfriend with herpes and admitted recklessly inflicting GBH because he knew he was infected prior to having sex with her.

Wound

Key case

In **C v Eisenhower 1983**, a wound was defined as being "any puncture of the skin". The case involved a child firing an air gun. The pellet hit V in the eye but did not break the skin. It was held that internal bleeding caused by the rupture of an internal organ was not a wound. Therefore, something that does not break the skin, such as an abrasion, bruise or burn would not amount to a wound.

Principle: Wound means a cut in the whole skin.

Examination pointer

You can see in **Eisenhower** that D was not guilty because the skin wasn't broken. This shows the importance of bringing the right charge because if the prosecution had charged him with GBH he could have been guilty, as the harm was serious. Remember this when applying the law in an examination scenario; you will be given the facts and will be expected to choose the appropriate offence.

Inflict and cause – is there a difference?

The *actus reus* of **s 20** is to unlawfully and maliciously wound or *'inflict'* grievous bodily harm. The *actus reus* of **s 18** is to unlawfully and maliciously wound or *'cause'* grievous bodily harm. In **Clarence 1888**, the word 'inflict' was held to mean that a prior assault was required, as for **s 47**. Other cases seem to have ignored this requirement. In **Wilson 1984**, the HL held that a person could be charged under **s 20** without an assault. They relied on the Australian case of **Salisbury 1976** where it was said that 'inflict' does not imply assault is needed. However it was said that the word 'inflict' did mean that *direct* application of force was needed. It was therefore narrower than the word 'cause'.

Evaluation pointer

This uncertainty has been clarified. Both **Salisbury** and **Wilson** were approved by the HL in **Ireland & Burstow 1997**. In the CA Lord Bingham had said it would be *"an affront to common sense"* to distinguish between the two offences in this way. The HL confirmed that liability for GBH could occur without the application of direct or indirect force, and rejected the argument that 'inflict' was narrower than 'cause'. Lord Hope made the statement in the opening quote, that the words 'cause' and 'inflict' may be taken to be interchangeable. **Clarence** was referred to as a "troublesome authority". In **Dica**, the CA again confirmed that there was no requirement of assault for a charge

52

under **s 20**. This seems sensible as there is no requirement, as in **s 47**, that an assault causes, inflicts or occasions the harm – only that D does.

A factor worth noting (as it was by the HL) is that the **1861 Act** consolidated several different Acts. Therefore, the difference in the two sections is not as significant as it would be had they been written at the same time.

One criticism is that if there is no requirement of assault in **s 20** then it is hard to justify convicting D of *assault* occasioning actual bodily harm as an alternative, as was confirmed again in **Savage & Parmenter 1992**.

Grievous bodily harm

This is commonly called GBH. In **Smith 1961**, grievous was interpreted by the HL to mean 'really serious'. In **Saunders 1985**, the CA held that the word 'really' was unnecessary. Thus, GBH includes *any* serious harm. In **Burstow 1996**, a campaign of harassment by D, which led to V suffering severe depressive illness, was charged under **s 20**. In the joint appeals to the HL in **Ireland & Burstow 1997**, the HL confirmed that psychiatric harm could come under **s 47**, **s 18** or **s 20**.

Serious harm is usually required, but note should be taken of **Bollom 2004**. A baby suffered bruising to several parts of her body and her mother's partner was charged with GBH. Although the CA substituted the conviction for one of ABH, it was made clear that bruising could amount to GBH if the victim was a young child. This means the age of the victim may be relevant in deciding the appropriate charge. Presumably, this argument could also be applied to an old or vulnerable person.

A wound may occur without GBH. Conversely, GBH may occur without a wound.

Example

Let's reconsider two cases we saw when looking at **s 47**.

In **Savage**, the glass broke and cut the other girl. This is technically a wound as the skin has been broken. She could have been charged with wounding under **s 20**. It would not be 'serious' harm though so no charge of inflicting GBH would succeed.

In the joint appeals of **Ireland & Burstow**, the HL said psychiatric harm could amount to GBH. This type of harm could not be a wound though.

Examination pointer

Look for clues in the scenario. If it refers to a cut then discuss wounding under either **s 18** or **s 20**. If it is only a small cut you could discuss **s 47**. If a serious internal injury is mentioned then discuss GBH. In all cases, the prosecution must establish a chain of causation. D's act must make a *significant contribution* to the wound or harm (see Chapter 2).

S 20 refers to "with or without any weapon or instrument". **S 18** refers to "by any means whatsoever". Remember these offences came from different Acts and were not written at the same time. It doesn't matter *how* D inflicts or causes the harm. However, the use of a weapon may help in establishing intent to cause serious harm, and so point you at **s 18**.

Mens rea

It is important to be able to identify the different *mens rea* in **s 18** and **s 20**. There are two differences: the type of *mens rea* and the type of harm that the *mens rea* relates to.

Both sections contain the word 'maliciously'. This does not mean spite or ill will, as we might view the word. As regards **s 20**, the CA interpreted it in **Cunningham 1957** as meaning intent or subjective recklessness (see Chapter 3). For **s 18**, it would appear that the word 'maliciously' is unnecessary. In **Mowatt 1968**, the judge said, "*In s 18 the word 'maliciously' adds nothing*".

Mens rea for s 20

As noted above this is intent or subjective recklessness. However, D need not intend or recognise the risk of serious harm. Intending or seeing the risk (*mens rea*) of *some* harm is enough as long as the result (*actus reus*) is serious harm. This was confirmed by the CA in **Mowatt** and later approved by the HL in **Savage & Parmenter 1992**.

Key case

In **Parmenter** D threw his baby into the air and caused GBH when he caught it. His argument that he lacked *mens rea* succeeded. He had not seen the risk of *any* injury (he'd done it before several times with older children) so he was not guilty.

Principle: The *mens rea* for **s 20** is intent or recklessness to inflict some harm, not serious harm.

It is only necessary to prove that D foresaw some harm *might* occur. It is not necessary to prove that D foresaw that some harm *would* occur. This point was confirmed in **DPP v A 2000**. Here a 13-year-old boy shot his friend whilst they were playing with two air pistols. His argument that he lacked *mens rea* was rejected. The case is similar to **C v Eisenhower 1983**.

In **Jones v First-Tier Tribunal 2011**, the CA held that for a charge of GBH there was no need to prove that the action was hostile. D had run in front of a lorry and the driver was injured. D argued he had no *mens rea* as he had only intended to harm himself, not anyone else. The CA held that it was foreseeable that harm could be caused to the driver of the lorry; therefore, the *mens rea* of recklessness could be proved for the **s 20** offence. In **Jones v FTT 2013**, the SC allowed D's appeal. The SC noted that the CA had decided that anyone running into a busy road must have at least seen the risk of some harm and, referring to **Parmenter,** held this was sufficient *mens rea* for **s 20**. However, the SC said that the question of whether D *himself* foresaw harm was a matter for the tribunal and not an appeal court, and reinstated the tribunal's decision

Evaluation pointer

S 18 and **s 20** involve *either* GBH *or* wounding. The first has been interpreted as 'really serious' harm (**Smith**), however wounding has been interpreted as an 'open cut' (**Eisenhower**), which could be quite trivial. The prosecution failed to prove D had inflicted a wound in **Eisenhower** because there was no open cut and thus no 'wound'. This case highlights the need to get the charge right. A charge of GBH could have succeeded. Another issue is that, as for **s 47**, the *mens rea* does not match the *actus reus*. For **s 20**, you need serious harm to have occurred, but the *mens rea* is only for *some* harm (**Mowatt**).

Application of mens rea for s 20

- Direct intent: It is D's aim to cause *some harm*

- Indirect intent: *Some harm* is a virtual certainty and D appreciates this

- Subjective recklessness: D recognises the risk of *some harm* and goes ahead anyway

Mens rea *for s 18*

The *mens rea* for **s 18** is specific intent, i.e., intent only. It was confirmed in **Belfon 1976**, where D had slashed someone with a razor, that recklessness was not enough, there must be intent to cause serious harm. **S 18** says *"with intent to do some grievous bodily harm"*. It was confirmed in **Parmenter** that for **s 18** D must intend *serious harm*. This is the vital difference and makes **s 18** much more serious, leading to a possible maximum life sentence. **S 20** carries a maximum of 5 years. In **Mair 2016**, the killer of the MP Jo Cox knifed a man who had tried to intervene when he saw the attack, causing serious injuries. He was found guilty under **s 18** (and of the murder). He was sentenced to life imprisonment for both offences.

In **Press & another 2013**, two soldiers were convicted of GBH under **s 18 OAPA** after attacking another two men at a burger stall. The CA confirmed that if D has taken alcohol (or drugs) the jury should ignore the alcohol and consider whether the act was accompanied by the required intent even in drink. The fact that the defendant was intoxicated does not constitute a defence. If intent had not been proved they would still have been guilty under **s 20** as they were at least reckless. **S 20** is a basic intent crime and voluntary intoxication is never a defence to a basic intent crime (one where recklessness suffices for *mens rea* – see under defences).

A further difference with **s 18** *mens rea* is that it includes intent to resist or prevent a lawful arrest. The problem with this is that it is added as an alternative to intent to cause GBH, so has been interpreted as meaning that if the situation is resisting or preventing an arrest, intent is only needed for that, not the harm. This is seen in **Morrison 1989** where D dived through a window resisting arrest and a police officer was badly cut. The CA upheld his conviction and held that it was enough that he intended resisting arrest. Regarding GBH, the word 'malicious' suggested that intent OR recklessness was enough, and he had been reckless.

Evaluation pointer

If **s 18** requires serious harm in both *actus reus* and *mens rea*, then arguably so should **s 20**. There is still a difference in the *mens rea* because **s 18** requires intent to be proved.

Another issue is sentencing. The maximum sentences for **s 20** and **s 18** are very different. The maximum for **s 20** is the same as **s 47**, i.e., 5 years. This seems strange. Life for **s 18** can be justified in that intent seriously to injure is also the *mens rea* for murder. Which charge is brought will depend on the chance factor of whether the victim dies or not. The same sentence for **s 47** and **s 20** is harder to justify. In **Parmenter**, the CA. noted there was an overlap between **s 47** and **s 20** but indicated that **s 20** was a more serious offence. The Law Commission proposes a maximum of 5 years for **s 47**, as now, but a maximum 7 years for **s 20**. This seems more realistic – but the reforms may be a long way off becoming reality.

A further recommendation by the Law Commission is that **s 18** would be 'intentional serious injury' and **s 20** would be 'reckless serious injury'. This would clear up the problem of the *mens rea*. It is arguably unfair to charge someone with GBH when the *mens rea* was only for some harm. A final criticism of the current law is that there are two different offences in each section. This makes four offences in all, which is unnecessarily complicated

The Commission notes that the Act is widely recognised as being outdated and that it uses archaic language. It also says that the structure of the Act is unsatisfactory; because there is no clear hierarchy of offences and the differences between **sections 18, 20** and **47** are not clearly spelt out.

Reforms are further discussed, along with the latest report from 2015, in the summary which follows this Chapter.

Application of mens rea for s 18

- Direct intent: It is D's aim or purpose to cause *grievous bodily harm*

- Indirect intent: *Grievous bodily harm* is a virtual certainty and D appreciates this

Which charge?

It was confirmed in **Savage 1991** that a jury could bring in **s 20** as an alternative verdict when someone is charged under **s 18** and **s 47** as an alternative to **s 20**.

If not, the conviction may be changed on appeal.

In **Bollom 2004**, the conviction for GBH under **s 20** was reduced by the CA to ABH under **s 47**.

Alternatively, D may put in a plea before or during the trial.

In **Topp 2011**, (unreported) a woman bit her boyfriend's testicles. He needed several stitches and she was charged with wounding with intent under **s 18**. Prior to the trial, she pleaded guilty to **s 20**, arguing she did not intend serious harm. The prosecution accepted the alternative plea.

Sometimes both charges are brought so the prosecution can be more confident of getting a conviction.

In **Hargreaves 2010**, D was in a taxi with her boyfriend and another man, all of whom had been drinking. She was in the back and was having an argument with her boyfriend, who was sitting in the front. He turned towards her and she kicked out at him, ramming a stiletto heel through his eye and into his brain. She was charged with both grievous bodily harm with intent under **s 18**, and an alternative charge of inflicting grievous bodily harm under **s 20**. (There would have been a conviction under **s 20** but she said that she had kicked out at him as she believed he was going to attack her, and pleaded self-defence. The defence succeeded so she was acquitted of both offences.)

Task 12

Mick threw a brick at Steve as he was riding down a country lane on his bicycle. The brick missed but Steve fell off his bike onto a sharp stone, causing a deep cut which needed several stitches. Explain the most appropriate offence and then apply the law to justify it.

Examination pointer

All this means you may need to discuss all three statutory offences. Explain the *actus reus* of either GBH or wounding as appropriate, using cases in support. Note carefully the difference in the *mens rea* as this may help you to decide which section is most appropriate. Thus if you go for **s 18**, explain and apply the law (with cases) but then say that if the prosecution can't prove intent to cause GBH then D may be convicted of **s 20** instead. If you go for **s 20**, you can then discuss **s 47** if you feel the harm may not be serious enough.

Terminology

Make sure you understand the following terms:

- **Grievous bodily harm – means serious harm**
- **Wounding – means cutting through the skin**

Summary

Actus reus	
Inflict or cause	Mean the same thing (Ireland)
Wound	Open cut (Eisenhower)
Grievous bodily harm	Serious harm (Smith/Saunders)
Mens rea	
S 20 Intent or recklessness	To cause some harm (Mowatt)
S 18 Intent only	To cause serious harm (Parmenter)

Links to the nature of law

Justice requires fairness and certainty and the lack of match between *mens rea* and *actus reus* in s 20 is not fair. The non-fatal offences have been the subject of much criticism and proposals for reform by the Law Commission. Again, these are covered in more detail in the summary following the next chapter.

Self-test questions

1. *How has 'wound' been interpreted?*
2. *How has 'grievous bodily harm' been interpreted?*
3. *Which cases can you use to support your answers to the above questions?*
4. *What is the difference in the mens rea between **s 20** and **s 18**?*
5. *What are the maximum sentences for **s 20** and **s 18** respectively?*

Answers to tasks and self-test questions are on my website at **www.drsr.org/publications/tasks.** For some interactive exercises, click on 'Free Exercises'.

The offences of assault and battery come from the common law, the others from the **Offences against the Person Act 1861**. Make sure you know the section numbers for these. Also, note the date of the Act. It is very old and is in need of reform. Reforms have been suggested but not implemented. Evaluation is dealt with in depth in The Bridge but you need to be able to evaluate the offences for AS as well as the A level so a shorter version follows this summary.

Note in particular the statutory offences where the *mens rea* doesn't match the *actus reus*. Make sure you understand the *mens rea* for each offence.

Examination pointer

You need to be accurate when discussing the *actus reus* and *mens rea* of these offences, so make sure you learn the definitions. Assault and battery are common law offences so it is cases which provide both the definitions and the principles of law. For ABH, GBH and wounding the law comes from a statute, (the **Offences against the Person Act 1861**), but as you know statutes have to be interpreted by judges. For these offences you need to learn the definitions and section numbers from the statute, and then make sure you know the cases which establish the various principles of law.

Assault

Actus reus: to cause the victim to apprehend *immediate* and unlawful personal violence – **Ireland**

Mens rea: intent or subjective recklessness to cause fear of harm – **Savage**

Battery

Actus reus: unlawful application of force to another – **Collins v Wilcock**

Mens rea: intent or subjective recklessness to apply force – **Venna**

Assault occasioning actual bodily harm under s 47 OAPA 1861

Actus reus: An assault (or battery) which causes harm – **Chan Fook**

Mens rea: intent or subjective recklessness for the assault or battery only – **Savage**

Malicious Wounding under s 20 OAPA 1861

Actus reus: unlawful and malicious wounding or inflicting grievous bodily harm – **C v Eisenhower / Saunders**

Mens rea: intent or subjective recklessness to inflict *some* harm – **Mowatt**

Wounding with intent under s 18 OAPA 1861

Actus reus: unlawful and malicious wounding or causing grievous bodily harm **C v Eisenhower / Saunders**

Mens rea – intent (only) to cause grievous bodily harm – **Parmenter**

Task 13

Match the principle to the case

Cases:

- **Wilson 1955**
- **Ireland 1996**
- **C v Eisenhower 1983**
- **Miller 1954**
- **Haystead 2000**
- **Smith1961**
- **Chan-Fook 1994**

Principles:

- **Silence may be enough for an assault**
- **Grievous means really serious harm**
- **Words may be enough for an assault**
- **A battery can be via another person**
- **Actual bodily harm is anything that causes personal discomfort**
- **Mere emotions such as fear, distress or panic are not enough for actual bodily harm**
- **Wound means an open cut**

Evaluation: Problems and proposals for reform of the non-fatal offences

The **Act** is very complicated and was written in 1861, so much of the language is obscure. Lawyers and juries have struggled to understand the complexities of the different offences. The courts also have difficulty interpreting words such as 'occasioning', 'actual bodily harm', 'grievous' and 'maliciously' as they are not used in the same sense today.

Assault and battery are outside the **Act**. Clarity would require all the offences to be together in one place. However, an alternative argument is that the common law can keep them up to date, as in **Ireland**.

The main problem is that the *actus reus* and *mens rea* do not always match, so that D can be liable for a result without intending or being reckless as to that result. This applies to **s 20** and **s 47**. This lack of correspondence between *actus reus* and *mens rea* is known as 'constructive liability'. It is called constructive liability because liability is constructed from the *actus reus* of one offence and the *mens rea* of another e.g., liability for assault occasioning actual bodily harm under **s 47** is constructed from the *actus reus* of **s 47** plus the *mens rea* of assault.

The Law Commission has produced proposals for reform over a very long period of time. In 1998 the government produced its own Bill incorporating most of the LC's recommended changes, but to date Parliament has not found time to debate the issues.

From the outset, the LC has pointed out that the Act is outdated and uses archaic language. Also that there is a lack of a clear hierarchy and the offences are not classified in a coherent way. In 2014, the

LC readdressed the issue and issued a consultation paper (a scoping paper), which noted that the frequent changes in the law had left it in an incoherent and confusing state. A report followed and was published in November 2015 (Report No. 361). The 2015 proposals are based on the 1998 Draft Bill.

The table which follow shows the proposals from the 1998 Bill. The offences are redefined and in all of them the *mens rea* matches the *actus reus*.

Name of proposed offence	Explanation of proposed offence	Current offence
Intentional serious injury	Clause 1: intentionally causing serious injury	**S 18**
Reckless serious injury	Clause 2: recklessly causing serious injury	**S 20**
Intentional or reckless injury	Clause 3: intentionally or recklessly causing injury	**S 47**
Assault	Clause 4: intentionally or recklessly applying force to or causing an impact on the body of another; or Intentionally or recklessly causing another to believe force is imminent	Common assault (assault and battery)

There are some minor amendments to the 1998 draft bill in the 2015 report. The first three offences (intentionally causing serious injury, recklessly causing serious injury and intentionally or recklessly causing injury) would be as above. Assault would also be as above, but renamed as 'physical assault' (currently battery) and 'threatened assault' or 'assault by threats' (currently assault).

The only real difference is the proposal of a new offence of causing minor injuries. This would fall between intentionally or recklessly causing injury and assault so would span Clauses 3 and 4 from the Draft Bill. It would include cases where the assault (whether physical or threatened) causes some injury, however minor but would not require *mens rea* for the injury, as for **s 47** now. However, it would be triable only in the magistrates' court, with a maximum sentence of 12 months.

There is more on the problems and proposals for reform in The Bridge as A level students need a little more depth. However, if you are keen to get a top grade at AS level you could look at this too.

Remember, if you plan to do the A level there is no need to take an external examination at the end of Year 1 and it won't count towards the A level. However, if, you are not 100% sure about doing the full A level you should do it, then you will have a law qualification at AS level.

There are two papers. Each paper represents 50% of the AS examination.

Paper 1: The English legal system (40 marks) plus criminal law (40 marks)

Paper 2: Law making (40 marks) plus tort (40 marks)

About the examination

The assessment objectives (AOs)

These apply to all A level courses and all examination boards. The examination will test you in the following ways.

AO1 tests your knowledge and understanding of the English legal system and legal rules and principles (40 marks)

AO2 tests your ability to apply legal rules and principles to given scenarios in order to present a legal argument using appropriate terminology (20 marks)

AO3 tests your ability to evaluate and analyse the legal rules, principles and concepts (20 marks)

You should be aware of these weightings so that you plan your time accordingly. A01 accounts for half the marks. The other two are even.

For specimen papers and mark schemes visit the OCR site at www.ocr.org.uk.

Types of question and apportionment of marks

For each paper, there are:

4 questions on the English legal system (Paper 1 with criminal law) or law-making (Paper 2 with tort) at 10 marks each. One of these will ask you to evaluate the law.

4 questions on the substantive (criminal law or tort) based on a scenario, at ten marks each. Three of these require you to explain and apply the law and one will ask you to evaluate the law.

All questions must be answered.

Overall there are 40 marks for the substantive law and 40 for ELS or law making. This makes a total for each paper of 80 marks.

Examination guidance

Application advice

Read the scenarios carefully to make sure you understand the questions.

Sometimes you will be directed to a specific offence and sometimes not. It may be necessary to discuss more than one as there is an overlap, however, if you are told to discuss a particular offence you cannot get marks for discussing any other offence(s).

S 18 and **s 20** clearly overlap, so unless directed to one or the other you may need to discuss both. There is also a close connection to attempted murder, as it is sometimes a matter of chance that V did not die, for example due to prompt medical treatment. In **R v Z 2017** (unreported), a Year 10 schoolgirl thought a school friend had been involved in some online bullying she had suffered. Telling her that she had a present for her she arranged a meeting, and while the girl shut her eyes and waited for the present Z stabbed her. Fortunately, the girl sensed something was wrong and opened her eyes, therefore managing to avoid a fatal wound. The knife went through her school blazer and shirt but only a short way into her body. Although not a deep cut there was a wound and Z admitted wounding under **s 20**. She intended at least serious harm so it could certainly be **s 18**. In the actual case the jury found that Z had sufficient *mens rea* for murder. As the girl had only survived because she jumped back Z was convicted of attempted murder.

Always read the questions carefully so you know which offence(s) to discuss.

Try to summarise the facts in a few words. This is valuable when time is short. The principle of the case is the important part, although you may need to discuss the facts briefly to show why you have chosen that particular case.

Example

In **Roberts 1971 and Pagett 1983**, the principle was that a foreseeable act will not break the chain of causation. If the scenario involves someone being injured when running away from the threat of an attack, **Roberts** is the most appropriate case. You don't need all the facts but should refer to the fact that she tried to escape an attack, and this was foreseeable. The principle of the case was based on this, i.e., a foreseeable act does not break the chain of causation. This case therefore supports a conclusion that the chain wasn't broken so D is guilty for the injury caused.

If you can't remember the name of a case that Is relevant don't leave it out but refer to it in a general way, e.g., 'in one decided case....' or 'in a similar case....'

You need to use *current* and *relevant* legal rules, which come from statutes or cases. **Key cases** highlight cases which are particularly important. Also use the **examination pointers** plus the **diagrams** or **summaries** at the end of each Chapter as a guide. An answer should be rounded off with a conclusion as to liability. This need not be a firm conclusion; it may not be clear-cut, especially where a jury may be making the decision. You should never start an answer with "D will be guilty of ... ." What you need to do is to:

Identify the appropriate area of law – this will tell the examiner you have understood the focus of the scenario and will shape your answer.

Apply the relevant rules in a logical way to the facts– this will be the substance of your answer. Define the offence(s) then take each part of the *actus reus* and *mens rea* in turn. Do this for each offence if there is more than one. If you do this logically you won't leave anything out. If the area is covered by a statute, quote the law from that statute accurately and with section numbers if possible.

Add a little more detail if there is a particular issue shown by the facts – there will often be something particular to focus on so look for clues in the given facts to see if you need more on anything, e.g., causation.

Support your application with relevant cases – only use cases which are relevant to the particular scenario, and only state those facts that are essential to show the examiner why you have chosen that case e.g., because the facts are similar.

Conclude in a way that is sustainable and supported by what you have said and the cases you used – it is useful to look back at the question at this point. If it says "Advise Mary …", then make sure that your answer does so. In your conclusion you should pull together the different strands of your answer and then say that based on that application "I would advise Mary that …".

Try to refer to the facts of a scenario as often as you can when applying the law. This indicates that you are answering the specific question and have a sound enough knowledge to know which cases are relevant to the particular facts. It also helps to keep you focused.

Evaluation advice

Essays require more discussion and evaluation of the law or legal issues. The **key criticisms** in the summaries are designed to help with this, along with the **evaluation pointers**.

In an essay question, you may need to form an opinion or weigh up arguments about a particular area of law or legal procedure. Try to balance any arguments by referring to more than one viewpoint. Also round off your answer with a short concluding paragraph, preferably referring back to the question. This shows the examiner you are addressing the specific question and not one you would have preferred to have been asked.

As with application of the law, you should try to take a logical approach. The beginning should introduce the subject matter, the central part should explain/analyse/consider advantages and disadvantages of it as appropriate, and the conclusion should bring the various strands of argument together with reference to the question set.

Here's a summary:

Application question

Identify the appropriate area of law	• *Show the examiner you have understood the focus of the scenario*
Apply the relevant rules in a logical way	• *Define the offence(s)* • *Take each part of the* actus reus *and* mens rea *in turn* • *Do this for each offence if there is more than one*
Add more detail	• *look for clues in the given facts to see if you need more on anything, e.g., causation*
Support your application with relevant cases	• *only use cases which are relevant to the particular scenario* • *only state those facts that are essential to show the examiner why you have chosen that case*
Conclude	• *Look back at the question* • *If it says "Advise Mary …", then make sure that you do* • *Pull together the different strands*

Evaluation question

Introduce the subject matter	• *Identify the area of law* • *State the main issue(s)*
Explain, Analyse, Consider	• *Advantages* • *Disadvantages* • *Either: take all the advantages and then all the disadvantages (AAA + DDD)* • *Or: take advantages and disadvantages one at a time (A-D + A-D + A-D etc.)*
Conclude	• Bring the various strands of argument together • Refer to the question set

Although this book covers criminal law, I have included the English legal system in this paper because that is what you will get in the real examination.

Task 14

For the AS examination the marks are evenly distributed between the English legal system and criminal law. There are 80 marks in total and a time of 1½ hours.

AS Level law

H015/01 The legal system and criminal law

Time allowed 1 hour 30 minutes

Section A

The legal system

Answer **all** questions

1 Explain negotiation and mediation as forms of alternative dispute resolution **[10]**

2 Describe the three tracks that a civil case may be allocated to **[10]**

3 Describe the role of juries in the criminal justice system **[10]**

4 Discuss the value of using juries in the criminal justice system **[10]**

Section B

Criminal law

Read the scenario and answer **all** the questions

Don, Frank, Sergei and Tom are at a disco. Frank has an argument with Sergei. He pulls out a knife and stabs Sergei in the arm. Sergei is taken to hospital where he has to have several stitches.

Meanwhile, Don sees Tom dancing with his girlfriend, he grabs Tom's jacket and pulls him off the dance floor. Tom lands on a table laden with drinks and cuts his hand slightly on some broken glass.

5 Explain the term *actus reus* in criminal law **[10]**

6 Advise how the law on the non-fatal offences against the person will apply to Frank **[10]**

7 Advise how the law on the non-fatal offences against the person will apply to Don **[10]**

8 Discuss the problems with the offence under **s 47** of the **Offences against the Person Act 1861** and how far reforms of this offence would achieve greater justice **[10]**

END OF QUESTIONS

Total: 80 marks

Answers to tasks and self-test questions are on my website at **www.drsr.org/publications/tasks.** For some interactive exercises, click on 'Free Exercises'.

66

This section contains more evaluation of the law so far, along with examples of the nature of law from the areas already covered. If you decide to continue your studies you will need to discuss the problems and proposals for reform in greater depth but you won't be studying the non-fatal offences again. Similarly you will need to discuss the nature of law in relation to what you have learned so far. This chapter therefore prepares you for the second year if you decide to carry on and gives you more evaluation of the law so far even if you don't.

The problems with the non-fatal offences clearly suggest that justice is not being achieved, especially in those offences where *mens rea* does not match *actus reus*. Justice and morality are also relevant to matters such as the thin-skull rule (**Blaue**) and voluntariness of conduct (**Leicester v Pearson**).

Evaluation of the non-fatal offences against the person and proposals for reform

In Chapter 1, we looked at the main principles of criminal law which included the correspondence principle and fair labelling. The criticisms in the summary plus the following problems can all be related to these principles. We have seen many problems whilst looking at the individual offences and it is clear the **Offences against the Person Act 1861** needs reform. There are also more general issues:

Language: the **Act** is very complicated and was written in 1861, so much of the language is obscure. Lawyers and juries have struggled to understand the complexities of the different offences. The courts also have difficulty interpreting words such as 'occasioning', 'actual bodily harm', 'grievous' and 'maliciously' as they are not used in the same sense today. This can result in conflicting case law and injustice. The word 'bodily' in **s 47** indicates some kind of physical harm but has been interpreted to include psychiatric harm. This may make sense but the statute should be able to be applied by the judges without having to stretch the language. The word 'maliciously' has been interpreted as meaning recklessly (**Savage & Parmenter 1992**). However, it appears in **s 18** as well as **s 20** and the *mens rea* for **s 18** is intent only. In **Parmenter,** the judge had difficulty explaining 'maliciously' to the jury. He said that it meant that it was enough that D *should have foreseen* that some harm might occur. This sounds very like objective rather than subjective recklessness. In fact, on appeal, this was said to be a misdirection. It highlights the fact that these words need to be clearly explained. If the law lacks clarity then it does not achieve justice. It is also hard for the courts to interpret the words and meaning in such an old Act with obscure language.

Common law: assault and battery are outside the **Act**. Clarity (and therefore justice) would require all the offences to be together in one place. However, an alternative argument is that the common law can keep them up to date. This happened in **Ireland,** where it was recognised that an assault could be via a telephone. It is also confusing that assault means two things. It is used to cover the two offences of assault and battery (as seen in **s 47** which refers to an assault but means assault and battery) and the actual offence of causing someone to apprehend violence.

Proposals for reform have been produced and Bills put before Parliament over a long period, but to date Parliament has not found time to debate the issues – see below under proposed reforms.

Task 15

Look back at the **Evaluation pointer** boxes in each chapter. Write some notes on these with case examples. Add your own thoughts. Then read through the reforms. Ask yourself whether the proposed reforms would solve any of the problems you have identified.

Keep these notes for revision and as a guide to an evaluation question.

So, there are plenty of problems. What is being done about them?

Background of proposed reforms

The Law Commission has been considering codification of the criminal law for some time. This was a huge task and so it was decided it would be better to work on a series of self-contained bills to deal with different parts of the criminal law. In 1993, the Commission produced a report (**No 218**) and draft Bill on the non-fatal offences against the person. This never received parliamentary time but in 1998, the government produced its own Bill incorporating most of the recommended changes, but again little happened. In 2014, the Commission readdressed the issue and issued a consultation paper (a scoping paper), which noted that the frequent changes in the law had left it in an incoherent and confusing state. A report followed and was published in November 2015. The 2015 proposals are based on the 1998 Draft Bill.

From the outset, the LC has pointed out that:

■ **The Act is outdated and uses archaic language**

■ **There is a lack of a clear hierarchy and the offences are not classified in a coherent way. They are not classified in order of seriousness, so that s 20 and s 47 differ in the seriousness of harm but not in the maximum sentence. The Law Commission proposes a maximum of 5 years for s 47, as now, but a maximum 7 years for s 20. S 18 would still carry a maximum of life.**

■ **The Act does not actually accord with current practice. This means that although a minor wound may legally be a wound it is likely to be charged under s 47. Similarly, a minor injury is legally s 47 but usually charged as an assault (battery).**

■ **As regards *mens rea*, the mental element is not clearly defined and the word malicious comes into both s 20 and s 18. In the first case, it is not explained and in the second case, it 'adds nothing'. In Mowatt 1968, the judge said, "In s 18 the word 'maliciously' adds nothing".**

The main problem is that the *actus reus* and *mens rea* do not always match, so that D can be liable for a result without intending or being reckless as to that result. This applies to **s 20** and **s 47**. This lack of correspondence between *actus reus* and *mens rea* is known as 'constructive liability'. It is called constructive liability because liability is constructed from the *actus reus* of one offence and the *mens rea* of another, e.g., liability for assault occasioning actual bodily harm under **s 47** is constructed from the *actus reus* of **s 47** plus the *mens rea* of assault. (Constructive liability is also seen in murder and 'constructive' manslaughter.) Any law which allows someone to be guilty of a more serious offence when the fault element was for a lesser offence can be said to be unjust.

The 2015 report makes the same points and it is also clear the LC would uphold the 'correspondence principle' and would abolish constructive liability for the non-fatal offences.

The LC points out that there are four different ways of committing the offence under **s 18** and suggests that resisting arrest should be a separate offence and not included in **s 18**.

The LC also refers to the problem caused by the different words of 'cause' and 'inflict' in **s 18** and **s 20**. The intention is to restructure the law and modernise and simplify the language. The LC suggests basing the reforms on the 1998 draft bill with some amendments.

The table which follow shows the proposals from the 1998 Bill. The offences are redefined and in all of them the *mens rea* matches the *actus reus*.

Name of proposed offence	Explanation of proposed offence	Current offence
Intentional serious injury	Clause 1: intentionally causing serious injury	S 18
Reckless serious injury	Clause 2: recklessly causing serious injury	S 20
Intentional or reckless injury	Clause 3: intentionally or recklessly causing injury	S 47
Assault	Clause 4: intentionally or recklessly applying force to or causing an impact on the body of another; or intentionally or recklessly causing another to believe force is imminent	Common assault (assault and battery)

In each case, the word 'causing' is used. The Bill also defines injury to include both physical and psychiatric harm.

Injury would include mental as well as physical harm, as long as it is a recognised psychiatric condition and also include disease. Note that there is no need for a prior assault for any of these offences (as there is currently for **s 47**). Nor is there a mention of the word 'wound'. The LC felt that wounding does not need to be a separate category as it can be an injury or a serious injury depending on the facts. As regards transmitting a disease it was felt this could come within causing injury (serious or otherwise) but if it could not then there should be a separate review of this area.

The 2015 proposals

The 2015 proposals are still based on the 1998 Bill, but with some minor amendments. The first three offences (intentionally causing serious injury, recklessly causing serious injury and intentionally or recklessly causing injury) would be as above. Assault would also be as above, but renamed as 'physical assault' (currently battery) and 'threatened assault' or 'assault by threats' (currently assault).

The only real difference is the proposal of a new offence of causing minor injuries. This would fall between intentionally or recklessly causing injury and assault so would span Clauses 3 and 4 from the Draft Bill. It would include cases where the assault (whether physical or threatened) causes some injury, however minor, but would not require *mens rea* for the injury, as for **s 47** now. However, it would be triable only in the magistrates' court, with a maximum sentence of 12 months.

I gave you a brief introduction to the nature of law concepts in Chapter 1 so you could start thinking about these concepts. Here is a bit more detail.

The nature of law (concepts)

The first paragraph is repeated from Chapter 1.

The word law in phrases such as criminal law, human rights law, contract law etc., refers to the substance of the law (hence these topics are called substantive law). The word law in a wider sense is a more elusive concept, as it relates to the nature rather than the substance of law (called non-substantive law). It involves consideration of what academics and Judges think the nature of law is (and what it should be). This in itself involves consideration of theories of law, such as law and justice, law and morality, the role of law in society in balancing competing interests and the role of law in keeping up with and regulating new technology. When considering the nature of law you need to look at the rest of your course from a different perspective.

The law plays a role in society by regulating behaviour and establishing social control. It punishes those convicted of a crime and compensates the victims of any civil wrongdoing. It also facilitates (e.g., by giving powers to form contracts or get married) and protects (e.g., by laws against theft and violence, and data protection laws). The law plays an important role in society not only in providing justice but also as a method of social control and of balancing competing interests (both public and private) to control the way society behaves. It sometimes involves enforcing moral as well as legal rules. Another role of law involves developing the law to keep up with new technology, either through the courts or by passing an Act of Parliament. These are all concepts of law, or legal theories.

Most people recognise the role of law in punishing offenders who are found to be at fault in criminal cases, but the law has a less obvious role in many other areas. The following are all real cases and provide examples of the role that the law plays in society in relation to the above concepts

I have included a range of examples in the table below, not just criminal cases. It should help you to see how to relate the substantive law in practice to the nature of law in theory, and to illustrate that there is an overlap between these concepts.

Case	Brief facts	The nature and role of law
Brown 1994 (See Chapter 7)	A criminal case where serious injuries had occurred during consensual sado-masochistic sex in private. Those involved were convicted of grievous bodily harm. A controversial case because they were all adults and no-one was forced.	In balancing the interests the law included the public interest (what was best for society) and also thought the moral wrong should be punished (society needs protecting from violent behaviour, even in private).
Re A 2001	A hospital sought a court order to allow an operation on Siamese twins to separate them. The result would be that one twin would die but without the operation they both would.	In granting the order the law had balanced many different interests. This not only included the people concerned but the public interest. The morality of the action also affected the decision in court. This shows the difficulty for the courts as society is divided on such issues.
Miller v Jackson 1977	A woman wanted the court to award an injunction to stop cricket being played nearby because she often had cricket balls landing in her garden.	In balancing the interests the court included the public interest and thought society would not be best served by granting an injunction to stop the cricket. The injunction was refused.
Murray v Express Newspapers 2008	The author of the Harry Potter books, JK Rowling, brought a case on behalf of her young son against a photographic agency for publishing secretly taken photographs of him.	The court had to balance the interests of the agency in freedom of expression against the child's right to privacy. The balance came down in favour of the child's right, and the court made clear each case would depend on its own facts and the decision could be different with an adult. This shows that in balancing interests the law is also protecting the vulnerable (the child).
Gemmell & Richards 2003 (See Chapter 3)	Two boys set light to some papers outside the back of a shop. Several premises were badly damaged. They were convicted of recklessly causing criminal damage by fire (arson) because the risk of damage was obvious to a reasonable person. Their ages were therefore not taken into account.	In order to achieve justice the HL overruled an earlier law and decided a person required a greater level of fault in order to be guilty of a crime. Thus to prove recklessness it must be shown that D is aware of a risk, but deliberately goes ahead and takes it. This shows the importance of proving fault in criminal law.

Some knowledge of these concepts is needed for you to understand how the links to the nature of law given in each chapter apply, so here is a brief description of each with a couple of views and/or comments as a taster, using cases from the table above.

Law and society

One role of the law is to do justice and in order to achieve justice the law may need to balance competing Interests. Another role of law is to regulate behaviour and the law will consider the interests of society when doing this.

If one person has a right (an 'interest') this often conflicts with the rights of another person, as in the **Murray** case in the table. In order to decide whose rights are to be enforced the courts must balance the competing interests to arrive at a decision. The balance is not only between private interests (as in **Murray**) but may be between public and private (as in **Miller v Jackson**). There may be several interests to balance, as in **Re A**, and the court may find the balancing act difficult – but that is part of the role of law, to consider difficult issues and make a decision as to what the legal position should be.

One view (that of Roscoe Pound) regarding competing interests is that law is an engineering tool which can be used to balance the different interests in society to achieve social control. However he believed that public interests should not be balanced against private ones because the public interest will always prevail; a case example is **Miller v Jackson**. When you look at cases consider what the interests involved are and how they conflict. Then consider whether the law achieved an appropriate balance (and therefore justice).

Law and morality

Both law and morals involve rules. As noted earlier, although they share many characteristics, there is a distinction between social rules and legal rules. The courts enforce the law, but not social rules. An important question is whether moral issues should be a matter for society alone, or whether the law should promote and/or enforce morality. A law which makes immoral behaviour illegal is promoting morality, engineering the way society behaves. If the law makes a decision in court based on morality it is enforcing morality, as in **Brown 1994**. There has been much debate on this subject and there are opposing views. Here are simplified versions of three:

Professor Hart says that law and morals are separate and the law should not be used to enforce morality. If a law is made using the proper procedures, it is a valid law even if immoral, and so it must be obeyed. This is positivism.

Lord Devlin said that law and morals are related and immoral acts, even in private, should be punished. Also, even if made using the proper procedures, if a law is immoral it is not a valid law and need not be obeyed. This is natural law.

John Stuart Mill said that the law should not normally be used to enforce morality but could if harm to others is involved. This is a type of positivism and also of utilitarianism (see under justice).

The decision in **Brown** was partly based on the fact that the acts were seen as immoral. Hart would see that as irrelevant, Devlin would not. Mill might go either way as harm was caused to others but it was by consent. The decision was only by a 3-2 majority so you can see that the Judges disagreed on this issue too. Note the overlap with justice. The three views above are all views on what justice involves.

Consider whether the law should be involved in what is essentially a moral issue. We live in a pluralist society with diverse views, so there is no 'shared morality'. What some people see as immoral, others do not (e.g., fox-hunting and smoking). What is regarded as immoral in one society, or in one time, may not be so in another (e.g., gay marriage, abortion and adultery). This makes legal involvement in morals a tricky issue, especially in controversial areas like euthanasia and enforced feeding for anorexics. **Re A** is another example of controversy. Many thought it was immoral to end a life by going ahead with the operation, but others argued that it would be more immoral not to separate the twins because both would eventually die.

Law and justice

One important role of the law is to achieve justice, so any of the cases in the table can be used to illustrate this concept. As you saw in Chapter 1, the rule of law requires fairness, and this is one meaning of justice, as is equality, another part of the rule of law. However, justice means different things to different people and as you can see from **Re A**, justice may be achieved for some but not all. There are different theories on what justice means and how it is achieved.

The three theories under 'law and morals' are theories of justice. Another theory of justice, called utilitarianism, is that justice is achieved when the 'greatest happiness' is achieved. A law which produces a lot of benefit would be a just law. Applying this to **Re A**, we can say that as the operation would save a life this was a big plus, so justice would be achieved by allowing it. However, if you look back to the natural law theory of justice, this is that it should have a moral content so an immoral law is not a proper law. On this view the decision in **Re A** did not achieve justice because it was immoral to operate knowing the other twin would die.

When you look at the case examples consider whether the law achieves justice, and by whose theory. You should also consider justice when studying the English legal system so that you can discuss whether the different legal institutions and procedures achieve justice.

Law and technology

As technology develops and new technologies arrive the law must be prepared to keep up. Obvious examples are internet and email scams, online abuse and cyber-crime in general. Other issues relate to data protection and privacy because these are harder to control with such easy access to information through the internet. The law will attempt to control how far personal information can be retained by government agencies, and the EU has led the way. The **Data Protection Directive 1995** outlawed indiscriminate and non-consensual retention of personal information and the **e-Privacy Directive 2002** built on this and extended its protection to people affected by the retention of electronic communications. Member states are not totally prohibited from retaining or using data but any derogation must be for security or prevention of crime and must also be both necessary and proportionate. This often connects to human rights law as in **Murray** above, where the right to privacy was at issue and there is no explicit right to privacy in UK law.

Let's finish on this by applying the above concepts to one example to see how the theory works in practice.

Example

R v R 1991, involved a man accused of raping his wife. They were separated and she had moved back in with her parents. He forced his way in to their house and assaulted her while attempting rape. At the time, rape within marriage was not against the law because a woman was deemed to have consented to sex purely by being married. The case went to the House of Lords (now the Supreme Court) on appeal.

The HL decided that rape within marriage was no longer acceptable. Although this was not about law and technology, it is an example of the law needing to keep up with change, in this case changing social attitudes. The judges presumably felt they achieved justice for the wife. Whether the man achieved justice is another matter. It is part of the concept of justice that the law is not retrospective and however wrong he may have been morally, at the time of the event it was not against the law. In making the decision the court exercised a form of social control. In order to do this it had to balance the competing interests of D (not to be guilty of what had at the time been a legal act) against those of his wife (to have the law's protection) and the wider public interest (violence can affect society as a whole). The public interest will usually prevail and here there was the added interest of the wife. The fact that the act was accompanied by violence showed a greater degree of fault, which may have tipped the balance against D. He should be punished (sanctioned) for his wrongdoing and society should be controlled so that this type of behaviour is eradicated. Finally, there is clearly a moral issue because the judges thought the law was wrong to allow an immoral act such as rape, even within marriage. However, Hart could say the decision should be based only on legal rules not morality, and that D should not have been punished for what was at the time a legal action, even if it was immoral.

On the other hand, Devlin might agree that he should be punished because the law which allowed rape within marriage was itself immoral and so not valid.

It is also arguable that an elected Parliament should decide on whether this type of act is against the law, not unelected judges. In fact, Parliament did act, after the event, and changed the law to match the decision.

A utilitarian would say this decision, and the later law by Parliament, achieved justice as a greater number of people benefit from the law prohibiting acts of violence, especially as (unlike **Brown 1994**) it was against the victim's wishes.

Evaluation pointer

As you saw in Chapter 1, an important role for the law is to uphold the rule of law. Another is to achieve justice. Both these require, among other things, equality, clarity and fairness. Any of the cases you see where the decision seems wrong on the facts, can illustrate a lack of fairness. Cases where there is inconsistency can illustrate a lack of clarity, and cases where those involved are not treated equally can illustrate a lack of equality. As you look at case examples bear this in mind. This will give you lots of material to illustrate a discussion of the nature of law in achieving justice, and will help you understand how the rule of law applies.

 Links to the nature of law from the AS law studied so far

The nature of law

Now you have had a better look at the nature of law, let's see how these concepts can link to what you have studied so far, with the emphasis on justice.

Actus reus

There are several cases which can be used to illustrate the various concepts of law. Here are a few of them.

One role of law is to provide justice and to punish those at fault. 'State of affairs' cases such as **Larsonneur 1933** and **Winzar v Chief Constable of Kent 1983** seem unjust because the Ds did not act voluntarily, so were not at fault. There is not usually a legal obligation to act even though there may be a moral one, so there is not usually liability where there is an omission to act rather than an act.

However, this rule changes where there is a duty to act, as in **Pittwood 1902**, **Stone and Dobinson 1977** etc. There is also a lower degree of fault in such cases but D may be liable for a serious crime such as manslaughter, and even murder (**Gibbins & Proctor**). The role of law is to provide justice and this is arguably unjust. The thin-skull rule also seems unjust because D may be guilty because of the victim's actions, as in **Blaue 1975**.

Mens rea

One role of law is to punish those at fault. Where the *mens rea* does not correspond with the *actus reus* this is known as constructive liability and it is not just law. D should only be liable where the

74

mens rea was for the offence actually committed. The role the law played in **Gemmell and Richards 2003** was a more just one. The HL confirmed that recklessness is subjective and that the **Caldwell** test was wrong. By overruling its previous decision and raising the level of fault required, the HL achieved a greater degree of justice.

Strict liability

Strict liability means liability without fault. This is a way of protecting society and is arguably just when applied to regulatory offences such as health and safety. However, it is less justifiable in offences which carry a social stigma, as in **G 2008**. It is also arguably immoral to make a person liable even though all care has been taken, as in **Shah**. As in most cases where the public interest is balanced against a private one, the public interest prevails (**Pound**). It is questionable whether this type of liability achieves justice.

The non-fatal offences

Constructive liability, where the *mens rea* does not correspond with the *actus reus*, is not just. The level of fault in such cases is lower than it should be. This occurs with both **s 47** and **s 20**. D should only be liable where the *mens rea* was for the offence actually committed, but under **s 47** D is liable for the more serious offence of causing actual bodily harm even though the *mens rea* was only for an assault or a battery. Cases such as **Roberts 1971** and **Savage 1991** illustrate this point.

Again, for **s 20**, the level of fault required is lower than it should be as liability for grievous bodily harm or wounding only requires that D had *mens rea* for causing 'some harm', not serious harm – **Mowatt 1968** illustrates this point. The role of law is to punish those at fault and to achieve justice, and it can be said that with constructive liability the law does neither of these adequately. In **Brown 1994**, the decision was partly based on morality and arguably this is not the role of law. However, the law balanced the interests of D with those of society and the decision favoured protecting society from immoral and violent acts. The fact that the **Offences against the Person Act** is so old means that the role the law plays is a difficult one. It is hard to achieve justice when the language and meaning of an Act is obscure. In **C v Eisenhower 1983**, he was found not guilty merely because the charge was wrong and there was no wound. Justice was not achieved. Refer back to the problems and reforms in the summary for more on this.

.

Appendix: Abbreviations

The following abbreviations are commonly used. In an examination you should write them in full the first time, e.g., write 'actual bodily harm (ABH)' and then after that you can just write 'ABH'.

General

Draft Code – A Criminal Code for England and Wales (Law Commission No. 177), 1989

CCRC Criminal Cases Review Commission

ABH actual bodily harm

GBH grievous bodily harm

D defendant

C claimant

V Victim

QBD Queen's Bench Division (of the High Court)

CA Court of Appeal

HL House of Lords

SC Supreme Court

Acts

S – section (thus **s 1** Theft Act 1968 refers to section 1 of that Act)

s 1(2) means section 1 subsection 2 of an Act.

OAPA – Offences against the Person Act 1861

In cases – these don't need to be written in full

CC (at beginning) chief constable

CC (at end) county council

BC borough council

DC district council

LBC London borough council

AHA Area Health Authority

J Justice

LJ Lord Justice

LCJ Lord Chief Justice

LC Lord Chancellor

AG Attorney General

CPS Crown Prosecution Service

DPP Director of Public Prosecutions

AG's Reference (No 6 of 1980) 1981 39

Airedale NHS Trust v Bland 1993 ....12, 14

Alphacell v Woodward 1972 30

Barnes 2004 39

Belfon 1976 51

Blake 1997 ....12, 31

Blaue 1975 ....18, 69

Bollom 2004 ....49, 52

Brown 1994 ....7, 47, 67, 69, 70

Burrell and Harmer 1967 39

Burstow 1996 49

C v Eisenhower 1983 ....48, 50, 70

Caldwell 1982 25

Chan-Fook 1994 43

Chua 2015 16

Clarence 1888 48

Collins v Wilcock 1984 38

Constanza 1997 36

Corbett 1996 17

Courtie 1984 42

Cunningham 1957 ....25, 50

Dica 2004 48

DPP v A 2000 50

DPP v K 1990 39

DPP v Ross Smith 2006 44

DPP v Smith 1960 21

Dytham 1979 13

Elliott 1983 25

Fagan v Metropolitan Police Commissioner
  1969 ....11, 14, 26, 39

Faulkner and Talbot 1981 38

G 2008 30

Gammon (Hong Kong) Ltd v AG of HK 1985 30

Gemmell and Richards 2003 ....25, 27, 70

Golding 2014 48

Hancock and Shankland 1986 22

Hargreaves 2010 52

Harrow LBC v Shah 1999 29

Haystead 2000 39

Ireland & Burstow 1997 ....35, 48, 49

Ireland 1996 ....35, 37, 44

Jackson 2006 31

Jones 1988 39

Jones v First-Tier Tribunal 2011 50

Jones v FTT 2013 50

Jordan 1956 16

K 2001 30

Larsonneur 1933 ....13, 14, 28, 69

Leicester v Pearson 1952 ....11, 14, 28

Madeley 1990 20

Mair 2016 51

Matthews and Alleyne 2003 23

Meade and Belt 1823 36

Meah v Roberts 1977 29

Mellor 1996 16

Miller 1954 43

Miller 1983 13

Miller v Jackson 66

Mohan 1975 21

Moloney 1985 21

Morrison 1989 51

Mowatt 1968 ....50, 63, 70

Nedrick 1986 22

Pagett 1983 ....16, 58

Pittwood 1902 ....12, 69

Press & another 2013 51

Prince 1875 30

R v R 1991 ....43, 68

R v Z 2017 57

Roberts 1971 ....16, 37, 44, 58, 70

Saunders 1985 49

Savage & Parmenter 1992 ....38, 44, 49, 50, 62

Savage 1991 ....52, 70

Savage1991 ....37, 42

Smedley's v Breed 1974 29

Smith 1961 49

Smith v Chief Superintendent of Woking
  Police Station 1983 36

Smith1959 15

Stone and Dobinson 1977 ....13, 69

Stringer 2008 23

Sweet v Parsley 1970 29

Taylor 2016 30

Thabo Meli 1954 26

Thomas 1985 ....35, 38

Topp 2011 52

Turbeville v Savage 1669.............................36

Venna 1976...40

Walker and Hayles 1990 23

White 1910 14

Williams & Davis 1992 17

Wilson 1955...36

Wilson 1984...48

Wilson 1996 ....43, 47

Winzar v Chief Constable of Kent 1983 13, 14, 28, 69

Woollin 1998 22

20770381R00047

Printed in Poland
by Amazon Fulfillment
Poland Sp. z o.o., Wrocław